# Also by Patrick Barry

## Books

*Editing and Advocacy: Volume 1*

*Good with Words: Speaking and Presenting*

*Good with Words: Writing and Editing*

*Notes on Nuance*

*The Syntax of Sports, Class 1: The Words under the Words*

*The Syntax of Sports, Class 2: The Power of the Particular*

*The Syntax of Sports, Class 3: The Rule of Three*

*The Syntax of Sports, Class 4: Parallel Structure*

## Online Courses

"Good with Words: Speaking and Presenting" (Coursera)

"Good with Words: Writing and Editing" (Coursera)

# PUNCTUATION
## and
# PERSUASION

Volume 1

PATRICK BARRY

**The materials in this book were first used in courses that Professor Barry taught at the University of Chicago Law School, the University of Michigan Law School, and the UCLA School of Law. Here's what students who have taken those courses have said about them:**

"Taking this course was an absolute pleasure. I know that I will be using the skills I learned well into the future."

"I really enjoyed (and am still enjoying) taking this course. Professor Barry provides a really well-structured and organized course that makes it easy to understand and fun to learn."

"I think that Professor Barry is a phenomenal teacher. I would recommend this class to everyone. Honestly, I wish I could take it again!"

"I really loved this class. I learned a lot about the 'hard skills' necessary for good writing and editing, including very concrete grammar and style tips that will absolutely help my writing. But I also learned a lot about the 'soft skills' that go into being a good editor. If you have a chance to take this class, you absolutely should."

"The material was incredibly useful. I have Professor Barry's voice in my head now (in a good way) every time I'm editing."

"Best instructor ever!"

"Professor Barry is a fantastic teacher, and the structure of this class is very artfully created."

"Professor Barry presented information to us in a way that was easy to digest and remember. His teaching style is superb. I'm already incorporating things I've learned in this class into my writing."

"This course has really improved my ability to be a persuasive writer. The daunting task of writing has come way more naturally since I've started to apply Professor Barry's advice."

"I will be recommending his courses to everyone!"

"Professor Barry is truly one of the best professors I have ever had. He perfectly balanced being challenging and being nurturing."

"Professor Barry made me a much better lawyer."

"Very clear. Very precise. Love it!"

"Professor Barry is one of my all-time favorite professors. He cares about developing not only our writing skills but also our personal and professional skills."

"I use my arsenal of Professor Barry teachings every day."

"Professor Barry is awesome. I would love to take another class with him if I could!"

"I feel like I really grew as a writer in this course."

"Professor Barry is AMAZING! I honestly cannot say enough good things about him. He provided great feedback on several drafts of my briefs and really helped the development of my writing."

"One of the best teachers I've ever had."

"This is the best course I have ever taken."

"Every time I write, I have Professor Barry lessons running in my head. They've made all the difference."

Published in the United States of America by
Michigan Publishing
Manufactured in the United States of America

DOI: https://doi.org/10.3998/mpub.12562794

ISBN 978-1-60785-778-5 (paper)
ISBN 978-1-60785-779-2 (e-book)
ISBN 978-1-60785-780-8 (OA)

An imprint of Michigan Publishing, Maize Books serves the publishing needs of the University of Michigan community by making high-quality scholarship widely available in print and online. It represents a new model for authors seeking to share their work within and beyond the academy, offering streamlined selection, production, and distribution processes. Maize Books is intended as a complement to more formal modes of publication in a wide range of disciplinary areas. http://www.maizebooks.org

*For everyone who has struggled with
commas—or any other punctuation mark.*

*If you aren't interested in punctuation, or are afraid of it, you're missing out on some of the most beautiful, elegant tools a writer has to work with.*

—Ursula K. Le Guin, *Steering the Craft: A Twenty-First Century Guide to Sailing the Sea of Story* (1998)

*I hope my email doesn't make
the next presentation.*

—Message from a law student after seeing the
clumsily punctuated emails of other
students used as examples in class

# CONTENTS

# CONTENTS

# INTRODUCTION

*Writing, much like the choice of what clothes we wear, is always a push-and-pull between personal style and other people's expectations.*

—Cecelia Watson, author of *Semicolon: The Past, Present, and Future of a Misunderstood Mark* (2019)

I often teach punctuation to my law students by asking them to imagine me arguing a case in court. My evidence is solid, I tell them. My analysis is sound. I speak fluidly and persuasively. The only problem: *I am wearing bright orange running shoes.*

I then ask the students to write down some thoughts they think might be going through the judge's head about my orange shoes as I make my case. To make the exercise more concrete, I actually wear a pair of orange running shoes to class, along with my otherwise normal courtroom attire of a suit and tie.

Sometimes I'll even jump up on a desk or table so that the shoes can be displayed in their full neon glory. Students typically respond with the following comments:

- "You look ridiculous."
- "Your shoes are distracting."
- "I can't take you seriously."

Nobody thinks I look professional.

I then put on the board a sentence from a legal brief submitted in an employment law case:

> The record never established what exactly the employer's reporting requirements are, therefore it is impossible to say objectively whether or not Ms. Lynn has violated them.

That's an orange shoes sentence, I explain. A judge who cares about punctuation—and the skillful use of language in general—might form the same opinions about the person who wrote it that the students formed about me when I was up on the table. The judge could even use some of the same words and phrases: "ridiculous," "distracting," "can't take you seriously."

The culprit is the comma. Commas are generally not strong enough to hold together what are essentially two separate sentences:

**Sentence 1:** "The record never established what exactly the employer's reporting requirements are."

**Sentence 2:** "It is impossible to say objectively whether or not Ms. Lynn has violated them."

But if you didn't know that or if you think, as the author of the sentence perhaps did, "Well, if I throw in a 'therefore,' I'll be okay," then you're going to look pretty foolish—not just in that sentence but in a lot of other things you write as well.

The reason: it's hard to fix mistakes you don't see.

\* \* \*

I'm not really worried, of course, about my students wearing orange running shoes to court or some other place where that type of footwear isn't appropriate. They all have access to mirrors that can help them catch inappropriate clothing choices. They can all notice—or at least have someone tell them—when their outfits might damage their credibility. But what they don't have are mirrors for their inappropriate writing choices. They lack reliable ways to quickly and confidently evaluate whether what they are sending out into the world is sufficiently polished and professional.

This short book can't provide that for them. Only a long-term investment in experimentation, quality feedback, and reflection can.

But what the book can provide is a set of common punctuation errors to avoid and possible solutions to consider. It can also serve as a helpful reminder, particularly for lawyers and law students, that our sentences often trigger consequential judgments—about our cases, about our clients, and about ourselves. "You don't have a lot of confidence in the substance if the writing is bad," the chief justice of the United States Supreme Court, John Roberts, once said of the briefs attorneys submit.

Which is why along with the commonly offered advice to "Dress for success," we might also want to keep in mind a second suggestion: "Punctuate to persuade."

# CHAPTER 1

# Comma Splices

*The comma splice is unnecessary; a brief pause between two related thoughts can be accomplished by a semicolon like the one in this sentence. A full stop separates two thoughts more cleanly. Unless you're being aphoristic ("Man proposes, God disposes") or intentionally seeking a loose-knit style, beware that a comma splice is probably not worth the readers it will irritate.*

—Robert Lane Greene, "The Dreaded Comma Splice" (2012)

The introduction to this book identified a link between punctuation and persuasion. It then offered an example from an employment law case that contained one of the more common punctuation issues I see when reviewing the writing of lawyers and other professionals: "comma splices."

> The record never established what exactly the employer's reporting requirements are, therefore it is impossible to say objectively whether or not Ms. Lynn has violated them.

I want to use a different example in this chapter, however, because I think it will help us more clearly see what comma splices are and how to more skillfully spot and use them. The example comes from the medium in which most of us do the bulk of our writing each day: email. Here it is:

> I really appreciate your willingness to help, I am excited to get more feedback from you!

The problem with this sentence is similar to the problem with the employment law sentence. The person who wrote it created a compositional crash between what are essentially two sentences:

**Sentence 1:** "I really appreciate your willingness to help."
**Sentence 2:** "I am excited to get more feedback from you."

To understand what I mean, it's helpful to think of an observation made by the writer Pico Iyer: "Punctuation marks are the road signs placed along the highway of our communication—to control speeds, provide directions and prevent head-on collisions."

A comma is simply not the appropriate "road sign" in the email the student sent. It's not strong enough. A better option would be a period, which you can think of as a stop sign:

I really appreciate your willingness to help. I am excited to get more feedback from you!

Or the person could have used a semicolon, which you can think of as a yield sign:

I really appreciate your willingness to help; I am excited to get more feedback from you!

But if our only protection is a comma, we are generally going to cause one of those head-on collisions that Iyer warns about.

I say "generally" because there are exceptions, as the journalist and English professor Ben Yagoda points out in *How to Not Write Bad*. "Comma splices are okay in rare cases," Yagoda notes, "including sentences where even a semicolon would slow things down too much." An example that might qualify appears in *Born a Crime* by the comedian Trevor Noah. He opts for a comma splice at the end of the following short description of his parents' contrasting characteristics: "My mom was wild and impulsive. My father was reserved and rational. She was fire, he was ice."

Notice, though, that Noah precedes that commas splice with two sentences that helpfully adhere to current grammatical conventions. ("My mom was wild and impulsive. My father was reserved and rational.") Demonstrating that you can follow a norm is a good way to build the credibility needed to break it.

You'll also see comma splices in advertising slogans. Here's one from the cosmetics company Avon:

Beauty is the journey, empowerment is the destination.

But unless it is clear to readers that you are using a comma splice on purpose, it can be risky to throw one in, particularly when a more formal style is expected. A legal brief, cover letter, investment prospectus, or other high-stakes document is probably not the time to get creatively casual with your punctuation.

**Additional Advice**

1. "Comma splices may be used deliberately to emphasize the relationship between two short parallel clauses or to create a rhetorical effect of speed, excitement, or informality, though the result is almost always a run-on sentence."

    —Richard Nordquist, "Comma Splices" (2020)

2. "You can correct a comma splice in four ways:
    - Separate the independent clauses into two separate sentences. Punctuate both sentences with periods.
    - Replace the comma with a semicolon or with a semicolon and a conjunctive adverb such as *however* or *furthermore*. (The conjunctive adverb is then normally followed by a comma.)
    - Replace the comma with a comma and a coordinating conjunction.
    - Make one of the clauses into a subordinate clause."

    —Leslie Perelman, James Paradis & Edward Barrett, *The Mayfield Handbook of Technical and Scientific Writing* (1997)

3. "Even Strunk and White recognized that a comma splice is sometimes the best choice. For example, where the clauses are repetitive and short, a comma splice can work well, especially if the tone is informal:

    *A comma splice isn't an error, it's an option.*
    *A comma splice isn't an error; it's an option.*
    *A comma splice isn't an error. It's an option.*
    *A comma splice isn't an error—it's an option.*
    *A comma splice isn't an error (it's an option).*
    *A comma splice isn't an error, so it's an option.*

Each alternative introduces a different emphasis. The comma, the weakest of the available marks, suggests the closest possible relationship between the two ideas. A semicolon provides a more formal way of conveying a close relationship. A period marks a definitive break (a full stop, in British parlance). A dash is abrupt and emphatic. A parenthesis presents the second clause as . . . (well, parenthetical). A conjunction implies a specific relationship between the two clauses.

Which alternative you choose will depend on context and tone."

—Russell Harper, "Comma Splices and
Run-On Sentences" (2019)

## Punctuation Practice: Spliced Starts

Here are some memorable opening sentences from works of fiction. Identify any that contain at least one comma splice.

A. "They shoot the white girl first."

—Toni Morrison, *Paradise* (1997)

B. "It was the best of times, it was the worst of times, it was the age of wisdom, it was the age of foolishness, it was the epoch of belief, it was the epoch of incredulity, it was the season of light, it was the season of darkness, it was the spring of hope, it was the winter of despair."

—Charles Dickens, *A Tale of Two Cities* (1859)

C. "Three men came out from under the low-browed facade of Mandeville College, into the strong evening sunlight of a summer day which seemed as if it would never end; and in that sunlight they saw something well fitted to be the shock of their lives."

—G. K. Chesterton, "The Crime of the Communist" (1935)

D. "I was born twice: first, as a baby girl, on a remarkably smogless Detroit day of January 1960; and then again, as a teenage boy, in an emergency room near Petoskey, Michigan, in August of 1974."

—Jeffrey Eugenides, *Middlesex* (2002)

E. "We are united, he and I, though strangers, against the two women in front of us talking so steadily and audibly across the aisle to each other."

—Lydia Davis, "On the Train" (2014)

**Answers Explained**

*Correct Answer*

The only sentence that contains a comma splice is the opening of *A Tale of Two Cities* by Charles Dickens. In fact, it contains a whole bunch of them!

*Wrong Answers Explained*

**Toni Morrison:** We learned that a comma splice occurs when you use a comma to connect what could essentially be two complete sentences. Morrison doesn't use a comma in her opening: "They shoot the white girl first." So there can't be a comma splice.

**G. K. Chesterton and Jeffrey Eugenides:** The Chesterton sentence and the Eugenides sentence both have some funky things going on with them, including a somewhat unconventional use of a semicolon. (We'll learn more about semicolons in Chapters 9, 11, and 12.) But neither passage contains a comma splice. There's no instance of a comma connecting what could essentially be two complete sentences.

**Lydia Davis:** Davis packs a lot of commas into her sentence. But none of them connect two complete sentences. So there's no comma splice. (We'll learn more about what counts as a full sentence in Chapter 2 when we take a look at "independent clauses.")

# CHAPTER 2

# "However"

*When "however" is used to join clauses within a sentence, it acts as a conjunctive adverb like "nevertheless," not as a coordinating conjunction like "but" or "yet." The conventions of punctuation thus require that it be preceded by a semicolon, as in "Main Street will be closed to traffic for the parade; however, the stores along it will remain open." Using a comma instead of a semicolon is likely to be perceived as a mistake. In our 2015 survey, 86 percent of the Usage Panel gave an unacceptable rating to the sentence "Main Street will be closed to traffic for the parade, however, the stores along it will remain open."*

—*American Heritage Dictionary*, "However" (2021)

We've now learned about the comma splice and how when you have two complete sentences—or, if you want to use the technical term, when you have two "independent clauses"—a comma is generally not strong enough, on its own, to link them together. For a better, more professional approach, we can look at two independent clauses the civil rights expert Michelle Alexander joins in *The New Jim Crow*, her highly acclaimed examination of mass incarceration:

**Sentence 1:** "We have not ended racial caste in America."
**Sentence 2:** "We have merely redesigned it."

Alexander doesn't use a comma to combine these clauses. She doesn't write, "We have not ended racial caste in America, we have merely redesigned it." Instead, she uses something much stronger: a semicolon.

> We have not ended racial caste in America; we have merely redesigned it.

We'll take a closer look at semicolons in Chapters 9, 10, and 12. The point now is simply to flag them as a possible fix for comma splices.

Another good fix is a period. Alexander, for example, could have written her sentence the following way: "We have not ended racial caste in America. We have merely redesigned it." Structurally, this "not" construction is precisely the approach the award-winning steak house Ruth's Chris takes in its marketing materials. Here is one of its slogans: "Quality is <u>not</u> a trend. It's our signature." The period fortifies the contrast.

The hotel company Marriott has used a similar tactic when advertising its line of Residence Inn properties, which are designed for longer stays, like a week or even a month: "It's <u>not</u> a room. It's a Residence."

Compare that with the decision the luxury watch company Rolex made to stick with a comma splice in an ad campaign featuring iconic figures such as Marlon Brando, Elvis Presley, Sophia Loren, and Martin Luther King Jr.: "It doesn't just tell time, it tells history." Or the choice the Stanford legal historian Thomas Grey made when describing two different accounts of the life of the early 20th-century United States Supreme Court Justice Oliver Wendell Holmes Jr.: "Both stories are selective, neither is false."

These comma splices don't seem like accidents; they seem intentional. But be careful about taking that kind of chance, especially when addressing audiences that may be particularly faithful to prevailing norms of punctuation. The risk of annoying someone who objects to comma splices is often greater than the reward you'll get for delighting someone who appreciates when they are skillfully deployed.

Also note that adding a "however" to a comma splice *doesn't* solve the problem. To demonstrate what I mean, let's take a look at an email I received from a law student. The student is informing me that he won't be able to attend an upcoming writing workshop:

Hi Professor Barry,

I would really like to attend the writing workshop, <u>however</u>, I cannot make it this Friday.

The note contains something to the left of "however" that could be its own sentence:

I would really like to attend the writing workshop.

And it contains something to the right of "however" that could be its own sentence:

I cannot make it this Friday.

Each of these units constitutes an "independent clause," the key elements of which are a subject, a verb, and a complete thought. It's called an "independent clause" because the clause can exist on its own. It doesn't need anything else to count as a sentence.

We'll compare "independent clauses" with "dependent clauses" in Chapter 13. For now, the important thing to understand is that when you have two independent clauses—two units that can stand alone as sentences—you can't just stick a "however" between them, or at least not without adding stronger punctuation marks than a comma.

Said differently: You can't connect independent clauses with just commas and a "however." That combination is not currently an acceptable way to hold two sentences together.

* * *

I say "currently" because attitudes on this point might change. And when attitudes change, conventions change. As Rudolf Flesch puts it in *The Art of Readable Writing*, "The point is that the rules of English usage are not immutable natural laws, but simply conventions among English-speaking people. If enough educated people insist on making a 'mistake,' then it isn't a mistake anymore and the teachers might as well stop wasting their time correcting it."

Daniel Tammet articulates this idea more succinctly in *Every Word Is a Bird We Teach to Sing*, his wide-ranging journey through the world of language and communication. "English," he explains, "never stops." What he means is that English is always evolving, always being changed, always being challenged and reformed.

Perhaps someday using "however" in the way my student did—as a technique for connecting two independent clauses with just a couple of commas—will be acceptable. Research by the linguists Lizzie Hutton and Anne Curzan has revealed a significant trend in that direction. Writers in the 21st century, they explain, are not confused about how to use the conjunctive adverb "however"; people have simply "reinterpreted the term's grammatical status in some constructions such that it functions as a coordinator between clauses."

That said, Curzan and Hutton themselves note that "for any of us who act as grammatical gatekeepers in our roles as copy editors and/or writing instructors, we may not yet be ready to allow 'however' through the gate as a coordinator with just a comma and no semicolon; the risk that the writer (or the copy editor) will be judged negatively remains too high." With that caution in mind, I'd likely advise the student who wrote the email about missing the writing workshop to include a semicolon along with the original comma:

> I would really like to attend the writing workshop; however, I cannot make it this Friday.

Or maybe go with a period and a comma:

> I would really like to attend the writing workshop. However, I cannot make it this Friday.

You might encounter some people who will object to placing "However" at the beginning of a sentence, but they're an increasingly small minority. According to the highly dependable *American Heritage Dictionary*, "It is sometimes claimed that one should not use 'however' to begin a sentence, but few writers consistently follow this rule."

Yet, as I often tell my law students when they graduate and start to work for judges, executives, and other power players who sometimes have their own way of doing things, "If your boss says not to start a sentence with 'however', don't start a sentence with 'however'—at least not in your first few months on the job, especially given that you can pretty easily move 'however' to a different part of the sentence and get the same, or even better, effect":

> I would really like to attend the writing workshop. I cannot make it this Friday, however.

I would really like to attend the writing workshop. I cannot, <u>however</u>, make it this Friday.

I would really like to attend the writing workshop. I, <u>however</u>, cannot make it this Friday.

In the next chapter, we'll return to the mechanics and strategy that go into finding the proper place for "however." We'll also learn the difference between adverbial conjunctions—which is what the particular type of "however" we've been looking at is called—and coordinating conjunctions, which are the connecting words "for," "and," "nor," "but," "or," "yet," and "so." Like "however" and other adverbial conjunctions, these coordinating conjunctions are notorious for causing some tricky comma issues as well.

## Additional Advice

usage of punctuation with 'however' may seem confusing;
er, the distinctions are straightforward.

' has several distinct uses. In all but one, it is an
vord that modifies a verb. . . . The other use of
s a conjunction."

—Mark Nichol, "How to Punctuate
with 'However'" (2013)

' means 'but' or 'in spite of that,' grammarians
dverb, and in that role it can be hard to
ights what precedes, it should follow the
ith something stated previously, as in

nost money; the Class of 1955,
ntage of contributors.

; we will not, <u>however</u>, accept

hrwald Cook, *Line by Line:*
*Your Own Writing* (1985)

begin with 'however',
you're required to
eates the emphasis

wever'?" (2018)

## Punctuation Practice: Historical Howevers

Below is a sentence written in the 18th century, a sentence written in the 19th century, and a sentence written in the 20th. Which of them conform to 21st-century standards of how to punctuate the word "however" like a professional? Select all that apply.

A. "The division of labour, <u>however</u>, so far as it can be introduced, occasions, in every art, a proportionable increase of the produc tive powers of labour."

—Adam Smith, *The Wealth of Nations* (177

B. "He clearly saw, <u>however</u>, the full force of the principle of selection."

—Charles Darwin, *The Origin of Species* (

C. "<u>However</u>, we obtain a new result of fundamental impo when we carry out the analogous consideration for a r light."

—Albert Einstein, *Relativity:*
*and the General Th*

D. None of the above.

### Answers Explained

**A + B. Adam Smith and Charles Darwin:** Correct! As we learned in this chapter, paired commas are not the professional choice when you are using the word "however" to connect two independent clauses; you would need either a semicolon and a comma or a period and a comma. But paired commas *are* the professional choice when you are using "however" to present just one independent clause, as Adam Smith and Charles Darwin both do in their sentences. (We'll learn more about independent clauses in future chapters.)

**C. Albert Einstein:** Correct! This chapter cautioned that some people may object to using "However" at the beginning of a sentence. You should definitely keep that in mind if your boss is one of those people. But the general consensus is that it is okay to start a sentence with "However."

**D. None of the above:** Incorrect. Each of the examples—Smith, Darwin, and Einstein—conforms with current conventions of how to punctuate the word "however" like a professional.

# CHAPTER 3

# Adverbial Conjunctions

*Like a few other adverbs—notably "therefore" and "otherwise"—"however" often plays a role in run-on-sentences. . . . They read something like this: "I wanted to go on the trip, however, there wasn't a slot available." One cure, of course, is a semicolon after "trip." But the better cure is usually to give the sentence an initial Although-clause: "Although I wanted to go on the trip, there wasn't a slot available."*

—Bryan Garner, *Garner's Modern English Usage* (2016)

I mentioned two terms at the end of the last chapter: "adverbial conjunctions" and "coordinating conjunctions." We're going to wait until Chapters 4 and 5 to cover coordinating conjunctions, which are the connecting words "for," "and," "nor," "but," "or," "yet," and "so." In this chapter, we'll stick to adverbial conjunctions.

Adverbial conjunctions are sometimes called "conjunctive adverbs," "sentence adverbs," or "subordinating adverbs." But whatever name you decide to use, keep in mind that there are many more adverbial conjunctions than there are coordinating conjunctions. The list you are about to see doesn't include the full set of adverbial conjunctions, yet it's almost three times as big as the total number of coordinating conjunctions, of which there are only seven.

## Adverbial Conjunctions

- accordingly
- additionally
- certainly
- consequently
- conversely
- furthermore
- hence
- however
- incidentally
- in contrast
- instead
- meanwhile
- moreover
- namely
- nevertheless
- otherwise
- rather
- similarly
- therefore
- thus

As far as using adverbial conjunctions, two especially helpful functions stand out:

*1. Adverbial Conjunctions Add Emphasis*

The adverbial conjunction "moreover" adds emphasis in the following excerpt from *Team of Rivals: The Political Genius of Abraham Lincoln* by the Pulitzer Prize–winning historian Doris Kearns Goodwin:

> To be sure, [Lincoln] had a melancholy temperament, most likely imprinted on him from birth. But melancholy differs from depression.

It is not an illness; it does not proceed from a specific cause; it is an aspect of one's nature. It has been recognized by artists and writers for centuries as a potential source of creativity and achievement.

Abraham Lincoln

<u>Moreover</u>, Lincoln possessed an uncanny understanding of his shifting moods, a profound self-awareness that enabled him to find constructive ways to alleviate stress and sadness.

### 2. Adverbial Conjunctions Communicate Contrast

Notice the shift that the adverbial conjunction "instead" brings about in the following snippet from another Pulitzer Prize winner, journalist Rebecca Skloot. It comes from the book for which she won that award: *The Immortal Life of Henrietta Lacks*.

Gey began sending Henrietta's cells to any scientist who might use them for cancer research. Shipping live cells in the mail—a common practice today—wasn't done at the time. <u>Instead</u>, Gey sent them via plane in tubes with a few drops of culture medium, just enough to keep them alive for a short time.

\* \* \*

The University of Wisconsin Writing Center has a helpful resource that identifies three additional ways to think about adverbial conjunctions:

- Adverbial conjunctions indicate a connection between two independent clauses in a sentence.
- Adverbial conjunctions link the ideas in two or more sentences.

- Adverbial conjunctions show relationships between ideas within an independent clause.

The resource can be found at https://writing.wisc.edu/handbook/grammarpunct/conjadv/. Pay special attention to the two tips at the end of it about how to punctuate adverbial conjunctions. The first tip focuses on something we introduced in the previous chapter, while trying to figure out what to do with the word "however":

> When [an adverbial conjunction] connects two independent clauses in one sentence, it is preceded by a semicolon and followed by a comma.

The second tip covers a wide variety of other scenarios:

> If [an adverbial conjunction] is used in any other position in a sentence, it is set off by commas.

As an example of this second tip, consider the following excerpt from Maya Angelou's memoir *I Know Why the Caged Bird Sings*:

> Weekdays revolved on a sameness wheel. They turned into themselves so steadily and inevitably that each seemed to be the original of yesterday's rough draft. Saturdays, <u>however</u>, always broke the mold and dared to be different.

Angelou surrounds her "however" with commas because the word is not connecting two independent clauses. It's simply breaking up a thought within a single independent clause. Her approach might have been different if she had decided to put "however" one word earlier. Then she would be connecting two independent clauses, either with a period or with a semicolon and a comma:

Maya Angelou

**Period:** "Weekdays revolved on a sameness wheel. They turned into themselves so steadily and inevitably that each seemed to be the original of yesterday's rough draft. <u>However</u>, Saturdays always broke the mold and dared to be different."

**Semicolon/Comma:** "Weekdays revolved on a sameness wheel. They turned into themselves so steadily and inevitably that each seemed to be the original of yesterday's rough draft; <u>however</u>, Saturdays always broke the mold and dared to be different."*

As usual, there are exceptions and judgment calls. I, for example, increasingly tell my law students to take out the commas if the adverbial conjunction is something like "therefore" and used for emphasis:

**Yes:** "The court should therefore grant our motion."
**No:** "The court should, therefore, grant our motion."

The two commas in the "No" version strike me as clunky. They slow down the concluding thought too much.

But more important than how you approach these stylistic decisions is simply recognizing the syntactic flexibility that adverbial conjunctions offer. If we bring back the sentence from Maya Angelou, we can see that "however" can be moved to various parts of the sentence, depending on what kind of rhythm you want to create. You can put "however" at the beginning of the sentence:

<u>However</u>, Saturdays always broke the mold and dared to be different.

You could put it at the end:

---

* Angelou had another option as well. She could have left "however" where it was and still used a semicolon and commas: "They turned into themselves so steadily and inevitably that each seemed to be the original of yesterday's rough draft; Saturdays, <u>however</u>, always broke the mold and dared to be different."

Saturdays always broke the mold and dared to be different, <u>however</u>.

You can also put it in different spots in the middle:

Saturdays always, <u>however</u>, broke the mold and dared to be different.

Saturdays always broke the mold, <u>however</u>, and dared to be different.

Take advantage of this versatility. The other kind of conjunctions—coordinating conjunctions—can't be moved around so easily. Yet as we'll see in the next chapter, they have their own special set of helpful qualities.

## Additional Advice

1. "Incidentally, the use of conjunctive adverbs is beneficial to not only waxing poetic but also to creating intelligent and high-quality content."

   > —Britainy Sorenson, "How to Use
   > Conjunctive Adverbs" (2020)

2. "Most of the time, problems occur when the writer uses a conjunctive adverb in the middle of a sentence when a coordinating conjunction is actually needed. But remember that conjunctive adverbs can be used in any part of a sentence."

   > —Indiana University of Pennsylvania Writing
   > Center, "Common Problems with However,
   > Therefore, and Similar Words" (2021)

3. "We swear that, despite their name, conjunctive adverbs are in no way related to tropical diseases.

   Instead, they are very useful when writing, and there are many more of them than we often remember.

   Conjunctive adverbs connect one thing to another in a descriptive way. For example: Everyone was raving about the puppy video; *consequently*, it went viral by the end of the day.

   While 'however' and 'therefore' are perfectly useful, knowing alternative conjunctive adverbs comes in handy."

   > —Naval Postgraduate School Graduate Writing
   > Center, "Conjunctive Adverbs" (2021)

## Punctuation Practice: The Checklist Manifesto

Atul Gawande is a surgeon at Brigham and Women's Hospital in Boston, a staff writer at the *New Yorker*, and a professor at both Harvard Medical School and the T. H. Chan School of Public Health. He is also the author of several best-selling books, including *The Checklist Manifesto*.

Below are four passages from that book. Which of them contain at least one adverbial conjunction? Select all that apply.

A. "What is needed, however, isn't just that people working together be nice to each other. It is discipline. Discipline is hard—harder than trustworthiness and skill and perhaps even than selflessness. We are by nature flawed and inconstant creatures. We can't even keep from snacking between meals. We are not built for discipline. We are built for novelty and excitement, not for careful attention to detail. Discipline is something we have to work at."

B. "Good checklists, on the other hand, are precise. They are efficient, to the point, and easy to use even in the most difficult situations. They do not try to spell out everything—a checklist cannot fly a plane. Instead, they provide reminders of only the most critical and important steps—the ones that even the highly skilled professional using them could miss. Good checklists are, above all, practical."

C. "We don't like checklists. They can be painstaking. They're not much fun. But I don't think the issue here is mere laziness. There's something deeper, more visceral going on when people walk away not only from saving lives but from making money. It somehow feels beneath us to use a checklist, an embarrassment.

It runs counter to deeply held beliefs about how the truly great among us—those we aspire to be—handle situations of high stakes and complexity. The truly great are daring. They improvise. They do not have protocols and checklists. Maybe our idea of heroism needs updating."

D. "Here, then, is our situation at the start of the twenty-first century: We have accumulated stupendous know-how. We have put it in the hands of some of the most highly trained, highly skilled, and hardworking people in our society. And, with it, they have indeed accomplished extraordinary things. Nonetheless, that know-how is often unmanageable. Avoidable failures are common and persistent, not to mention demoralizing and frustrating, across many fields—from medicine to finance, business to government. And the reason is increasingly evident: the volume and complexity of what we know has exceeded our individual ability to deliver its benefits correctly, safely, or reliably. Knowledge has both saved us and burdened us."

### Answers Explained

**A. Correct!** The first sentence contains the adverbial conjunction "however" ("What is needed, <u>however</u>, isn't just that people working together be nice to each other").

**B. Correct!** This passage contains two adverbial conjunctions: "on the other hand" and "instead" ("Good checklists, <u>on the other hand</u>, are precise" and "<u>Instead</u>, they provide reminders of only the most critical and important steps—the ones that even the highly skilled professional using them could miss. Good checklists are, above all, practical").

**C. Incorrect.** There are multiple coordinating conjunctions in this passage ("but" and "and"), but there are no adverbial conjunctions.

**D. Correct!** The first sentence contains the adverbial conjunction "Nonetheless" ("<u>Nonetheless</u>, that know-how is often unmanageable. Avoidable failures are common and persistent, not to mention demoralizing and frustrating, across many fields—from medicine to finance, business to government").

# CHAPTER 4

# Coordinating Conjunctions

*I was signed to Columbia Records as a solo artist, so the band performed on Bruce Springsteen records. But live, I wanted the collective identity and living representations of the characters who populated my songs. It was James Brown and His Famous Flames, Buddy Holly and the Crickets—and that "and" was really important. It said there was a party going on, a meeting taking place, a congregation being called forth. YOU WERE BRINGING YOUR GANG! So, live we would be Bruce Springsteen and the E Street Band.*

—Bruce Springsteen, *Born to Run* (2016)

Coordinating conjunctions create a number of comma issues. But before we identify the key ones, let's review what coordinating conjunctions actually are. They can be remembered using the following tidy mnemonic: FANBOYS.

For
And
Nor
But
Or
Yet
So

The general purpose of coordinating conjunctions is to connect words, phrases, and even whole clauses. Their job is to, as the grammarian Constance Hale explains in *Sin and Syntax*, "hold equivalent things in balance":

> A coordinating conjunction might hold together grammatically parallel words (naughty *but* nice) or parts of a list (X, Y, *and* Z). It might also conjoin two phrases playing parallel roles in a sentence ("I'm so broke, I'll have a garage sale *and* hawk all my heirlooms."), or keep distinct clauses together.

Where people run into problems is picking the punctuation that accompanies coordinating conjunctions. One particularly important convention to be aware of is when you have two independent clauses connected by a coordinating conjunction: in those situations, it's generally a good idea to include a comma.

You can see this convention in a sentence from *The Man Who Mistook His Wife for a Hat* by the British neurologist Oliver Sacks. Sacks asks a patient who seems to be having trouble accurately perceiving images to look at a picture of the Sahara Desert and describe what he sees. Sacks's reaction to the patient's wildly off-base description gives us a chance to see the coordination conjunction "but" in action:

> I must have looked aghast, but he seemed to think he had done rather well.

Notice the comma Sacks includes before the "but." You wouldn't include that if the sentence instead pivoted on one of the adverbial conjunctions we learned about in the last chapter. You wouldn't write, "I must have looked aghast, <u>however</u> he seemed to think he had done rather well." The reason: a comma plus an *adverbial conjunction* is not strong enough to connect independent clauses.

Oliver Sacks

But a comma plus a *coordinating conjunction* is a much different story. That combination is indeed strong enough to connect independent clauses. You don't need a semicolon. You don't need a period. You don't need anything beyond a standard comma.

Keep in mind, though, that I didn't say that a coordinating conjunction *alone* is strong enough to connect two independent clauses. A comma is an essential part of the compositional equation.

So here's a quick tip: If you are unsure whether a comma goes before "but" or any other coordinating conjunction, simply look to what comes after it. If what you see can stand alone as a sentence—if, in other words, you spot a second independent clause—a comma is typically the professional choice. If not—if what you see cannot stand alone as a sentence—no comma is generally needed.

I'm hedging a bit, because plenty of skilled writers and well-edited publications frequently deviate from this convention, as we'll see in Chapter 5.

**Additional Advice**

1. "A coordinating conjunction is a word that joins two elements of equal grammatical rank and syntactic importance. They can join two verbs, two nouns, two adjectives, two phrases, or two independent clauses."

   —Catherine Traffis, "What Is a
   Coordinating Conjunction?" (2017)

2. "We use *so* . . . to introduce clauses of result or decision:
   - I got here late. It was a long journey, so I'm really tired now.
   - You are right, of course, so I think we will accept what the bank offers.
   - It's much cheaper with that airline, isn't it, so I'll get all the tickets for us with them."

   —*Cambridge Dictionary*, "So" (2021)

3. "As a conjunction between clauses or sentences, the semantics of *yet* are a bit like *but* or *however*, indicating a contrast. What's more, *yet* can hook up with *and*, as in this example:

   I studied that problem for years, and yet I never came close to the right solution.

   *For* is an even more flexible word. As a preposition, its meaning includes doing something on someone's behalf (*building a deck for them*), specifying rewards or deserts (*receive an award for work, punishment for misdeeds*), indicating support or advocacy (*I'm for Roosevelt*), or designating an amount (*a bill for $100*). As a conjunction, *for* has a meaning that overlaps with the subordinating *because*, though it is more formal in register. But unlike *because*, *for* only occurs after another clause. Consider this 1883 example from the *Oxford English Dictionary*:

> This is no party question, for it touches us not as Liberals or Conservatives, but as citizens.

The *for* clause cannot be moved to the front, though with *because*, either order of clauses is possible. And while all of the other FANBOYS are able to begin sentences, the conjunction *for* is quite rare in that position."

—Edwin Battistella, "Conjunction Dysfunction" (2020)

**Punctuation Practice: FANBOYS**

1. The following entry is taken from *The Elements of Style* by William Strunk Jr. and E. B. White:

   > **Conjunction:** *A word that joins phrases, clauses, or sentences. The coordinating conjunctions,* ___, ___, ___, ___, ___, ___, ___, *join grammatically equivalent elements.*

   Use the words in the box below to fill out the seven blanks:

   | for | moreover | neither |
   |-----|----------|---------|
   | and | yet      | nor     |
   | but | or       | so      |

2. The Colombian writer Gabriel García Márquez, who won the Nobel Prize in Literature in 1982, was a journalist before he became a novelist, and he continued to write nonfiction until his death in 2014. The passage below appears on the first page of one of those pieces of nonfiction, his 1996 book *News of a Kidnapping*:

   She looked over her shoulder before getting into the car to be sure no one was following her. It was 7:05 in the evening in Bogotá. It had been dark for an hour, the Parque Nacional was not well lit, and the silhouettes of leafless trees against a sad, overcast sky seemed ghostly, <u>but nothing appeared to be threatening</u>.

   The underlined portion of the passage is _____.

   Gabriel García Márquez

A. an independent clause, so the comma before the coordinating conjunction "but" is appropriate

B. an independent clause, so the comma before the coordinating conjunction "but" is <u>not</u> appropriate

C. a dependent clause, so the comma before the coordinating conjunction "but" is appropriate

D. a dependent clause, so the comma before the coordinating conjunction "but" is <u>not</u> appropriate

## Answers Explained

1.  The seven coordinating conjunctions are "for, and, nor, but, or, yet, so." They fill out the mnemonic FANBOYS.

    The word "neither" is a different kind of conjunction called a "correlative correction." (Another one of those is "either.") The word "moreover" is an example of the "adverbial conjunctions" we learned about in Chapter 3.

2.  The correct answer is A: "an independent clause, so the comma before the coordinating conjunction 'but' is appropriate." We learned in this chapter that a comma is the standard choice when a coordinating conjunction is used to connect two independent clauses.

# CHAPTER 5

# Coordinating Conjunctions (Deviations)

*Bob Gottlieb told me that he was always inserting commas into [Toni] Morrison's sentences and she was always taking them out.*

—Hilton Als, "Toni Morrison and the Ghosts in the House" (2003)

We left off our discussion of coordinating conjunctions with the following observation about skilled writers: they often deviate from the convention that says a comma goes before a coordinating conjunction when that coordinating conjunction connects two independent clauses.

A good example appears in the novel *Rabbit Redux* by John Updike, an author who enjoyed the writing process so much that he once said that he would have created labels on ketchup bottles if that had been the only writing job he could get. The main character in the novel, Harry "Rabbit" Angstrom, is explaining to his son what it's like to realize, in middle age, the disheartening discrepancy between what you think you can do athletically and what your body can actually deliver:

John Updike

> It's a funny feeling . . . when you get old. The brain sends out the order and the body looks the other way.

According to the convention, a comma should go before the word "and":

> It's a funny feeling . . . when you get old. The brain sends out the order, and the body looks the other way.

But Updike leaves that comma out. Not because he's ignorant and unprofessional. He's considered one of the most precise and erudite writers of the 20th century.

He leaves the comma out because he *can* leave it out. Conventions about punctuation are not ironclad laws of the universe. You don't always have to follow them, particularly if you can show, in the surrounding sentences, that you know what you're doing and are exceptionally careful with how you use language.

Said differently, *deliberate* deviations from convention are fine so long as your readers know you are in fact being deliberate. But *accidental* deviations—deviations that leave people wondering whether you are even aware of the conventions—well, those are the ones we'll definitely want to address.

## Additional Advice

1. "Writing is a negotiation between the rules of grammar and what the writer wants to say. Beginning writers need rules to make themselves understood, but a practiced writer gives color, personality, and emotion to writing by bending the rules."

   —John Seabrook, "Can a Machine Learn to Write for the *New Yorker?*" (2019)

2. "I like to use as few commas as possible so that sentences will go down in one swallow without touching the sides."

   —Florence King, *Reflections in a Jaundiced Eye* (1989)

3. "Rules and informal rules don't exist for their own sake; they're not sacred. Every so often, we must be ready to abandon a rule in favor of an act that would serve ourselves or the world better. And since grammar is a thing made up of rules that we sometimes need to violate in order to produce the actual effects we have in mind, it holds training value for us on this front. Being somewhat venturesome with a technically incorrect but tonally appropriate punctuation mark calls into play much the same dynamic that any thoughtful risk-taking involves."

   —Lawrence Weinstein, *Grammar for a Full Life: How the Ways We Shape a Sentence Can Limit or Enlarge Us* (2020)

**Punctuation Practice: Positive Deviance**

In "10 'Grammar Rules' It's OK to Break," the psychologist and language expert Steven Pinker identifies several questions that can help determine if a grammar "rule" is worth following. Here are a few:

- Has the rule been respected by the best writers in the past?
- Is it respected by careful writers in the present?
- Do attempts to fix a sentence so that it obeys the rule only make it clumsier and less clear?

To open yourself up to this kind of "positive deviance"—particularly when it comes to punctuation—write down at least two punctuation "rules" that you sometimes intentionally break. You might also try writing down two that you think should rarely (or possibly never) be broken. It can be at once instructive and freeing to separate the deviance you permit from the deviance you don't.

To help you generate your list, here are three rules from *The Elements of Style*, a book that continues to shape modern American writing habits perhaps more than any other publication, even though it was originally released all the way back in 1920. According to the Open Syllabus Project, which tracks what college students across the United States are assigned to read, *The Elements of Style* appears on more syllabi than any other text.

## 1. Do Not Join Independent Clauses with a Comma

If two or more clauses, grammatically complete and not joined by a conjunction, are to form a single compound sentence, the proper mark of punctuation is a semicolon.

> *Stevenson's romances are entertaining; they are full of exciting adventures.*

*It is nearly half past five; we cannot reach town before dark.*

It is of course equally correct to write the above as two sentences each, replacing the semicolons with periods:

*Stevenson's romances are entertaining. They are full of exciting adventures.*

*It is nearly half past five. We cannot reach town before dark.*

**2. Place a Comma before a Conjunction Introducing a Coordinate Clause**

*The early records of the city have disappeared, and the story of its first years can no longer be reconstructed.*

*The situation is perilous, but there is still one chance of escape.*

**3. A Participial Phrase at the Beginning of a Sentence Must Refer to the Grammatical Subject**

*Walking slowly down the road, he saw a woman accompanied by two children.*

The word "walking" refers to the subject of the sentence, not to the woman. If the writer wishes to make it refer to the woman, he must recast the sentence:

*He saw a woman accompanied by two children, walking slowly down the road.*

# CHAPTER 6

# "Language Is Rich, and Malleable"

*Punctuation was developed by stages [that] coincided with changing patterns of literacy, whereby new generations of readers in different historical situations imposed new demands on the written medium itself.*

—M. B. Parkes, *Pause and Effect: An Introduction to the History of Punctuation in the West* (1992)

The previous chapter identified one way that skilled writers deviate from comma conventions: they'll sometimes decide not to include a comma before a coordinating conjunction that connects one independent clause with another independent clause. We'll now identify a second way: including a comma even when there's no second independent clause.

A good example can be found in *A Poetry Handbook* by the American poet Mary Oliver. Here's the deviating sentence: "Language is rich, and malleable." According to the convention, a comma would only be needed if, after the first independent clause ("Language is rich"), there were a second independent clause to the right of the coordinating conjunction "and."

But there's not. There's just the word "malleable": "Language is rich, and <u>malleable</u>."

Yet Oliver nevertheless includes a comma—and I'm glad she does. The comma adds a helpful delay to the sentence. When you get to the words "and malleable," it's almost like being treated to an unexpected gift.

A similar thing happens in the book *In Other Words* by Jhumpa Lahiri. Describing the type of conversational partner she is looking for as she tries to learn to speak Italian, Lahiri writes the following sentence: "I need someone with whom I can struggle, and fail."

Before you imitate Lahiri, however, remember that she has the benefit of a Pulitzer Prize and many other awards on her résumé. If she departs from a convention, readers are likely to assume she did so on purpose—not out of ignorance.

Jhumpa Lahiri

The same might not be true of you, especially if you are corresponding with someone for the first time. Which is why I tell my students to play things safe, at least initially. After they build up some credibility—after they demonstrate that they're skilled linguistic custodians—they'll have more leeway to experiment. Even someone like the American poet E. E. Cummings, who broke all kinds of writing conventions (including sometimes not capitalizing his name), certainly knew what those conventions were. He studied Latin and Greek in high school and then gradu-

E. E. Cummings

ated magna cum laude from Harvard, after which he stuck around to earn a master's degree in English literature.

It's tough to imagine forging that kind of academic path without the ability to meet formal expectations.

## Additional Advice

1. "Modern readers will be disconcerted to see [Jane] Austen sticking a comma between a subject and verb or strewing dashes apparently at random. But as Sutherland herself noted in an earlier book, Austen often used punctuation to signal the rhythms of speech rather than the grammatical structure."

   —Geoff Nunberg, "Jane Austen:
   Missing the Points" (2010)

2. "I sometimes ignore the rules about commas although generally follow convention and adhere to the advice in Strunk and White. Punctuation is for clarity and also emphasis, but I also feel that, if the writing warrants it, punctuation can contribute to the rhythm and music of the sentence. You don't get permission for this, of course; you take the liberty."

   —James Salter, quoted by Mary Norris in *Between You & Me: Confessions of a Comma Queen* (2015)

3. "And yet we find many instances in which great writers break all the rules of grammar. . . . James Baldwin, for example, loves run-on sentences, many of which (but not all) appear as comma splices. For me, these are instances where the writer is not so much breaking the rules as they are simply remaking them in the image of their own text. Baldwin isn't making grammar errors; he is making a new grammar for himself."

   —Christian Kiefer, "How Does Garth Greenwell
   Make Such Wonderful Sentences?" (2020)

**Punctuation Practice: Rules Are Made to Be (Skillfully) Broken**

Which of the following passages contain a comma that deviates from the convention regarding commas and coordinating conjunctions? Select all that apply:

A. "This is the year she discovered pot, and sex."

—Nick Paumgarten, "Id Girls" (2014)

B. "Lately, the Sea of Polls is deeper than ever before, and darker."

—Jill Lepore, "Politics and the New Machine" (2015)

C. "The sheer quantity of brain power that hurled itself voluntarily and quixotically into the search for new baseball knowledge was either exhilarating or depressing, depending on how you felt about baseball. The same intellectual resources might have cured the common cold, or put a man on Pluto."

—Michael Lewis, *Moneyball* (2003)

D. "He was Irish, and illegal."

—Edward Delaney, "The Drowning" (1994)

## Answers Explained

Each of the passages contains a comma that deviates from the convention regarding commas and coordinating conjunctions. None, however, strike me as mistakes. Instead, the authors all seem to want to build in a rhetorical delay, like you might get if the comma were switched to a dash:*

- "This is the year she discovered pot—and sex."
- "Lately, the Sea of Polls is deeper than ever before—and darker."
- "The sheer quantity of brain power that hurled itself voluntarily and quixotically into the search for new baseball knowledge was either exhilarating or depressing, depending on how you felt about baseball. The same intellectual resources might have cured the common cold—or put a man on Pluto."
- "He was Irish—and illegal."

Compare each of those alternatives to the effect of removing the comma and following the coordination-conjunction convention:

- "This is the year she discovered pot and sex."
- "Lately, the Sea of Polls is deeper than ever before and darker."
- "The sheer quantity of brain power that hurled itself voluntarily and quixotically into the search for new baseball knowledge was either exhilarating or depressing, depending on how you felt about baseball. The same intellectual resources might have cured the common cold or put a man on Pluto."
- "He was Irish and illegal."

I'll leave it up to you to decide which punctuation choice works best. My goal is to expand your overall menu of options.

---

* We'll cover dashes in Volume 2 of *Punctuation and Persuasion*.

# CHAPTER 7

# Conjunctions Affect Other Conjunctions

*On occasion we write a sentence that isn't, in fact, correct, but it sings. And the question is: Would you rather be the ornithologist or the bird?*

—Colum McCann, *Letters to a Young Writer* (2017)

We've now covered two deviations from convention. The type identified in Chapter 6 involved skilled writers sometimes including a comma before a coordinating conjunction even though that conjunction does not connect independent clauses. One of the examples we highlighted came from *In Other Words* by Jhumpa Lahiri: "I need someone with whom I can struggle, and fail."

I want to offer an additional example. It appears in a judicial opinion written by John Roberts, the Supreme Court justice mentioned back at the beginning of this book. He is describing a hypothetical situation:

> Suppose Congress enacted a statute providing that every taxpayer who owns a house without energy efficient windows must pay $50 to the IRS. The amount due is adjusted based on factors such as taxable income and joint filing status, and is paid along with the taxpayer's income tax return.

Focus on the second sentence, the one that ends with the words "and is paid along with the taxpayer's income tax return":

> The amount due is adjusted based on factors such as taxable income and joint filing status, and is paid along with the taxpayer's income tax return.

Chief Justice John Roberts

If we were only concerned with following the conventions of punctuation, we might remove the comma in front of "and." The reason: what comes after "and" cannot stand alone as a sentence. It's not an independent clause.

But notice what would happen if we made that edit. There's a chance that the separation between the first part of the sentence ("The amount due is adjusted based on factors such as taxable income and joint filing status") and the second part of the sentence ("and is paid along with the taxpayer's income tax return") might be harder for readers to discern. The whole thing might just blend together:

> The amount due is adjusted based on factors such as taxable income and joint filing status and is paid along with the taxpayer's income tax return.

Adding the comma helps clarify the division, especially given the presence of the other "and" in the sentence:

> The amount due is adjusted based on factors such as taxable income <u>and</u> joint filing status, <u>and</u> is paid along with the taxpayer's income tax return.

I often remind my students that punctuation affects other punctuation. A dash in one part of a sentence or paragraph should influence whether you decide to use another dash in a different part of the sentence or paragraph. Micro-level edits need to be viewed within macro-level contexts.

The example from Justice Roberts highlights a related relationship: conjunctions affect other conjunctions. The first "and" in his sentence ("taxable income <u>and</u> joint filing status") complicates the decision to follow or deviate from the comma conventions that govern conjunctions when you get to the second "and" ("<u>and</u> is paid along with the taxpayer's income tax return"). Having just a single conjunction would make the choice a lot easier.

* * *

I obviously don't know if Justice Roberts was making any of these calculations when he crafted his sentence. Nor do I know whether everyone who reads the sentence will think he made the right choice. My main hope is that you keep sentences like it in mind as you continue to navigate (1) the sometimes tricky relationship between punctuation and persuasion and (2) the not uncommon tension between clarity and convention. As the longtime editor Harold Evans suggests in *Do I Make Myself Clear? Why Writing Well Matters*, "We should respect grammatical rules that make for clarity, but never be scared to reject rules that seem not to."

## Additional Advice

1. "Grammar exists to make written language coherent from one person to the next, so if adding or deleting a comma is going to change the meaning of your sentence, go with the structure that says what you want it to. If you don't really see the difference or don't care, go with the default rules you were taught."

—Kristen Csuti, "'Because' Is a Coordinating Conjunction. Fight Me." (2019)

2. "Too often, people think of commas purely in terms of right and wrong, correct and incorrect, grammatical and ungrammatical. Sometimes, though, comma placement is a matter of choice. In such cases, the decision to use a comma depends on the writer's intention."

—Christopher Altman, "Stylistic Commas: To Comma or Not to Comma?" (2013)

3. "Your sentences shouldn't leave your reader hyperventilating from the constant shallow breaths that over-punctuation requires. Nor should they be gasping for breath at the end of a long, unpunctuated sentence. (Consider yourself responsible for your readers' cardiovascular health.)"

—Kim Cooper, "Tips on Grammar, Punctuation, and Style" (2021)

**Punctuation Practice: Conjunction Congestion**

The sentence below was written by a first-year law student as part of a self-assessment exercise. It contains some tough-to-navigate congestion: three uses of the conjunction "and" in the same tight space.

> I think this technique will help me construct stronger <u>and</u> more nuanced arguments <u>and,</u> in the long run, break me out of my habitual patterns of thinking <u>and</u> push me to think more outside the box.

Try to repunctuate the sentence in a way that reduces this conjunction congestion. Feel free to add, change, or even remove any other words you want. Sometimes the delete button can solve what might otherwise seem like a punctuation headache.

**Answers Explained**

Here are a few possibilities for decongesting the student's sentence, although other options could certainly work as well:

- I think this technique will help me construct stronger, more nuanced arguments <u>and</u>, in the long run, break me out of my habitual patterns of thinking.
- I think this technique will help me construct stronger <u>and</u> more nuanced arguments; it might also, in the long run, break me out of my habitual patterns of thinking <u>and</u> push me to think more outside the box.
- I think this technique will help me construct stronger and more nuanced arguments. It might also, in the long run, break me out of my habitual patterns of thinking <u>and</u> push me to think more outside the box.

# CHAPTER 8

# Starting Sentences with "And" or "But"

*Everybody agrees that it's all right to begin a sentence with "and," and nearly everybody admits to having been taught at some past time that the practice was wrong.*

—*Merriam-Webster Dictionary of English Usage*, "Is It Ever Okay to Start a Sentence with 'And'?" (1994)

One of the most common questions I get from students about coordinating conjunctions such as "And" or "But" is, "Can I use one to start a sentence?" The answer is an emphatic "Yes!"

Benjamin Dreyer, the chief copy editor at the publishing behemoth Random House and the author of the best-selling book *Dreyer's English*, dismisses the prohibition against starting a sentence with "And" or "But" as one of the "Great Nonrules of the English Language." Great writers start sentences with "And" or "But" all the time, he notes. So the rest of us should feel free to as well, if that choice will improve the reader's experience.

Dreyer does, however, offer the following caveat:

> An "And" or a "But" (or a "For" or an "Or" or a "However" or a "Because," to cite four other sentence starters one is often warned against) is not always the strongest beginning for a sentence, and making a relentless habit of using any of them palls quickly. You may find that you don't need that "And" at all. You may find that your "And" or "But" sentence might easily attach to its predecessor sentence with either a comma or a semicolon.

He adds in a footnote that "as a copy editor, I'm always on my guard for monotonous repetition, whether it's of a pet word—all writers have pet words—or a pet sentence construction. Two sentences in a single paragraph beginning with the same introductory term, especially 'But,' are usually one sentence too many."

I'll include my own caveat, particularly if you are working for someone who is a stickler for one of these "nonrules." Just because you *can* start a sentence with a conjunction doesn't mean you *should*.

Writing is about consistently making good decisions. Sometimes starting a sentence with "And" or "But"—or any of the other coordinating conjunctions—will be a good decision. Sometimes it won't.

A useful way to learn the difference is to pay special attention to when skilled writers use a coordinating conjunction to start a sentence. Does that sentence come at the beginning of a paragraph? Does it come at the end? How long is the sentence that comes immediately before the one that starts with the conjunction? How about the one that comes immediately after? Is there another sentence nearby that starts the same way?

In the courses I teach, I institutionalize this practice through a "Good Sentences" assignment. Each week students read from a curated collection of quality writing.* The topics vary. History, business, technology, politics, literature, science—all kinds of things. But the task is always the same: find your favorite sentence and retype it word by well-crafted word.

Copying and pasting are not allowed. Students have to write the sentence as if they were composing it themselves. That way, they start to internalize the rhythm and structure of a thoughtfully arranged sequence of words—including those sequences that begin with "And" or "But."

---

* You can access the "Good Sentences" digital library at the following website: http://libguides.law.umich.edu/goodsentences. You should also be able to find it if you google "Good Sentences Michigan Law."

## Additional Advice

1. "I always see some shocked faces when I tell a classroom of college students that there is nothing wrong with beginning a sentence with the word *and* (or for that matter, the words *but*, *because*, or *however*).

   I encourage them not to take my word for it, but to look it up, so I refer them to Ernest Gowers' 1965 revision of *Fowler's Dictionary of Modern English Usage*, which explains that the idea is 'a faintly lingering superstition.' I also often suggest *Garner's Modern American Usage*, which calls it a 'rank superstition.' Superstitions don't age well, apparently. Even Wilson Follett's stuffy *Modern American Usage* calls the rule 'a prejudice [that] lingers from the days of schoolmarmism rhetoric.' William Safire included it in his book of 'misrules' of grammar, and Strunk and White didn't mention it as a problem at all. So there."

   —Edwin Battistella, "It's Fine to Start
   Sentences with 'And'" (2016)

2. "The idea that 'and' must not begin a sentence, or even a paragraph, is an empty superstition. The same goes for 'but.' Indeed either word can give unimprovably early warning of the sort of thing that is to follow."

   —Kingsley Amis, *The King's English* (1997)

3. "And God said, Let there be light: and there was light."

   —"Genesis 1:3," King James Bible (1611)

**Punctuation Practice: AP Advice**

The *AP Stylebook* is made by and for journalists, but many businesses and other organizations follow it as well. ("*AP*" stands for "*Associated Press*.") Here is its advice on starting a sentence with a conjunction:

> There's no AP Stylebook rule against starting a sentence with a conjunction. And it works well in some instances. But don't overuse it. Or readers will be _____.

Take a shot at filling in the word you think goes in the blank. Then note how many of the sentences in the passage start with a conjunction.

**Answers Explained**

The word that goes in the blank from the *AP Stylebook* is "annoyed":

> There's no AP Stylebook rule against starting a sentence with a conjunction. And it works well in some instances. But don't over-use it. Or readers will be <u>annoyed</u>.

As for how many of the sentences start with a conjunction, the number is three out of four:

> There's no AP Stylebook rule against starting a sentence with a conjunction. <u>And</u> it works well in some instances. <u>But</u> don't over-use it. <u>Or</u> readers will be annoyed.

# CHAPTER 9

# Be Kind to Semicolons

*The semicolon was born in Venice in 1494.*

—Cecelia Watson, "The Birth of the Semicolon" (2019)

We've spent a lot of time focusing on independent clauses. We'll soon move on to dependent clauses, but first I want to highlight another option you have when trying to connect the independent ones.

Consider the following pair of independent clauses from George Eliot's *Middlemarch*, one of the most revered novels in English literature:

- **Independent Clause 1:** "Dorothea quite despises Sir James Chettam."
- **Independent Clause 2:** "I believe she would not accept him."

George Eliot

We already know from previous chapters that one option would be to use a coordinating conjunction and a comma to connect these clauses, given that each can stand alone as a sentence:

> Dorothea quite despises Sir James Chettam, so I believe she would not accept him.

We also know that a second option would be to connect the clauses with a semicolon, an adverbial conjunction, and a comma:

> Dorothea quite despises Sir James Chettam; consequently, I believe she would not accept him.

Let's now cover a third option. It's actually the option Eliot herself chose: ditch the adverbial conjunction, ditch the comma, and just use a semicolon.

> Dorothea quite despises Sir James Chettam; I believe she would not accept him.

The added benefit of this option is that it shows the principal use of semicolons. They connect independent clauses.

With a few exceptions, you can test whether you are using a semicolon correctly by first looking to the left and right of it. If you see something that can stand alone as a sentence to the left of the semicolon and you see something that can stand alone as a sentence to the right of the semicolon, you're generally going to be in good shape, at least in terms of mechanics.

In terms of strategy, however, things get trickier, especially given that some people find semicolons at best unnecessary and at worst annoying. I used to work with a wonderful lawyer who mocked them as "creative punctuation." The word "creative" wasn't a compliment.

More famously, the writer Kurt Vonnegut suggests that all semicolons do is "show you've been to college." And in *Between You & Me: Confessions of a Comma Queen*, Mary Norris, who is a copy editor at the *New Yorker*, notes that "there is no mark of punctuation so upper-crust as the semicolon."

But one of the reasons I chose a sentence by George Eliot as our example is that she's actually been praised for her use of semicolons. Here's how one commentator, the journalist and teacher Ben Yagoda (we talked about him when discussing comma splices in Chapter 1), describes her skill with them:

Kurt Vonnegut

George Eliot was a semicolon virtuoso as well, recognizing it as a piece of punctuation that allows a gradual landing from a thought and take off to another one, rather than the abrupt and sometimes bumpy full stop of a period.

Being able to perform that kind of smooth "landing and takeoff" can be incredibly helpful, particularly if you are trying to connect a related set of ideas.

So yes, don't overuse semicolons. And yes, be aware that some people get really irritated by semicolons. But please do at least learn how they work. When deployed at the right time, in the right way, to the right people, they really can be quite effective.

A writing website created by Princeton University captures this point nicely. "Be kind to the semicolon," the site advises. "It may never win a popularity contest, but it has a place in every writer's toolbox."

## Additional Advice

1. "Used well, the semicolon makes a powerful impression; misused, it betrays your ignorance."

   —Mary Norris, *Between You & Me: Confessions of a Comma Queen* (2015)

2. "William James's paragraphs, as lucid and unpretentious as can be, are divided and subdivided, as intricately structured as the anatomical diagrams he includes in 'Psychology: Briefer Course.' Semicolons, along with exclamation points and dashes and whole sackfuls of commas, are, for him, vital tools in keeping what he called the 'stream of thought' from appearing to the reader as a wild torrent."

   —Ben Dolnick, "Semicolons: A Love Story" (2012)

3. "Think of the semicolon as a long comma, or a wimpy period."

   —Merrill Perlman, "To Semicolon, or Not to Semicolon" (2015)

## Punctuation Practice: Semicolon Standards

1. **True or False:** A semicolon is the same as a comma splice.
2. **True or False:** A semicolon can function like a period.
3. **True or False:** A semicolon can function like an adverbial conjunction.

**Answers Explained**

1. **False.** A semicolon is <u>not</u> the same as a comma splice. Both connect independent clauses, but a semicolon does so in a way that conforms with convention. A comma splice, on the other hand, does so in a way that deviates from convention, as we learned in Chapter 1.

2. **True.** A semicolon <u>can</u> function like a period. Both connect independent clauses in a way that conforms with convention. Consider the example from Mary Norris in the "Additional Advice" section:

   > Used well, the semicolon makes a powerful impression; misused, it betrays your ignorance.

   Technically, Norris could have used a period:

   > Used well, the semicolon makes a powerful impression. Misused, it betrays your ignorance.

   But stylistically, the tighter connection created by the semicolon achieves the desired rhetorical effect.

3. **False:** A semicolon can sometimes be paired with an adverbial conjunction, as we saw with one of the modifications to the sentence from George Eliot's *Middlemarch* earlier in this chapter. (I've underlined the adverbial conjunction.)

   > Dorothea quite despises Sir James Chettam; <u>consequently,</u> I believe she would not accept him.

   Alternatively, you can decide to get rid of the adverbial conjunction and just go with the semicolon:

Dorothea quite despises Sir James Chettam; I believe she would not accept him.

But what you (generally) can't do is substitute an adverbial conjunction for a semicolon. So the following construction, where "consequently" tries to play the role of a semicolon, wouldn't work:

Dorothea quite despises Sir James Chettam consequently, I believe she would not accept him.

We'd need to put the semicolon back in:

Dorothea quite despises Sir James Chettam; consequently, I believe she would not accept him.

# CHAPTER 10

# Punctuation Affects Other Punctuation

*By allowing the reader a chance to rest, a semicolon, for example, can take the pressure off a period, making it no longer feel like a distant object on the horizon.*

—Noah Lukeman, *A Dash of Style* (2006)

In the previous chapter, we looked at semicolons and their primary use as a way to connect independent clauses. Knowing that—as well as what we learned in Chapters 4 and 5 about coordinating conjunctions—we can generate a helpful equation. It has three linked parts:

Semicolon = Period = (Comma + Coordinating Conjunction)

To see how this equation works, let's return to the *Middlemarch* sentence we've been using and imagine it punctuated in three different ways:

**Semicolon:** Dorothea quite despises Sir James Chettam; I believe she would not accept him.

**Period:** Dorothea quite despises Sir James Chettam. I believe she would not accept him.

**Comma + Coordinating Conjunction:** Dorothea quite despises Sir James Chettam, so I believe she would not accept him.

Each of these options is functionally equivalent. They all communicate the same core message while also complying with current conventions of punctuation.

Once we realize that, we can also realize something else: we have a considerable amount of choice when it comes to style and strategy. Sometimes we'll want to separate our ideas with the clean, staccato clarity of a period—the punctuation mark that has the power to, in the words of the Norwegian writer Karl Ove Knausgaard, come down "like a mountaineer's cleat." Other times we'll want to establish a more fluid connection, opting instead for the continuity created by combining a comma with a coordinating conjunction.

There's also a third option. We could choose a hybrid approach. Some staccato, some fluidity. If that's the case, the right way to go is probably with a semicolon.

Factored into all these decisions, of course, should be an awareness of which punctuation marks already appear in the surrounding sentences. Are there too many semicolons nearby? Did you recently use a comma and coordinating conjunction?

One way to get a sense of this ratio is to assess your own punctuation portfolio. So the "Punctuation Practice" part of this chapter will give you a chance to take something you've written and then count the number of each type of punctuation mark you see on a particular page, in a particular section, or even throughout the whole document. The right punctuation for an isolated sentence might be the wrong punctuation for one that is connected to a bunch of other sentences.

Said differently: punctuation affects other punctuation.

**Additional Advice**

1. "Overuse of any punctuation mark tells us something about ourselves, in the same way overuse of any object does."

    —Philip Cowell, "What Overusing Exclamation Marks Says about You" (2017)

2. "I've noted before the risks of missteps, confusion or awkwardness in the use of dashes. Even if the dashes are correct and the syntax intact, we should avoid overdoing the device. It can seem like a tic; worse yet, it can indicate a profusion of overstuffed and loosely constructed sentences, bulging with parenthetical additions and asides."

    —Philip B. Corbett, "Dashes Everywhere" (2011)

3. "Did 19th- and early 20th-century writers sprinkle semicolons without any sense of propriety or limits? Or were there rules for semicolons that are obscure to us now? After looking at passages from T. S. Eliot, Henry James, George Eliot and Jane Austen, Mr. Nunberg at last discovered the old law of the semicolon: A semicolon that wants to dominate another semicolon in the same sentence must wait for the end of the sentence; and then it can act like a colon, trumping the rest; the last semicolon gets the last laugh."

    —Sarah Boxer, "If Not Strong, At Least Tricky: The Middleweight of Punctuation Politics" (1999)

## Punctuation Practice: Punctuation Portfolio

This exercise gives you a chance to create the "punctuation portfolio" mentioned earlier in the chapter. Think of it as eloquence-driven empiricism.

**Step 1:** Find a document that you've written that is at least a thousand words. If you can grab something longer than that, great. You'll benefit from having a large sample size.

**Step 2:** Guess the punctuation portfolio of the document. How many periods do you think you used? How many commas? How many semicolons?

Also consider punctuation marks we haven't learned about yet and won't be getting to until a later volume of *Punctuation and Persuasion*. These include colons, dashes, ellipses, exclamation points, and question marks. Skilled writers deploy each judiciously.

**Step 3:** With your estimated punctuation portfolio nearby, determine your actual punctuation portfolio. To speed up the process, use Ctrl+F or some similar Find function on your computer to search for each individual mark. Or if you are working with a paper version of the document, simply count the ones you see. This method will take more time, but it will also give you a more intimate look at your specific punctuation distribution.

**Step 4:** Compare your estimated punctuation portfolio with your actual punctuation portfolio. Are you surprised by the discrepancy (if there is one)? Are there certain punctuation marks that you use more than you thought? Less than you thought? Are there ones that you don't use at all but might want to in the future? Are there any that you want to significantly cut back on?

**Step 5 (Optional):** Find a few documents written by other people to use as benchmarks, something to gauge how your punctuation portfolio matches up against the writing of people you admire. If you're a lawyer, grab some well-written briefs, contracts, or judicial opinions. If you're a journalist, check out the latest issue of your favorite magazine or newspaper.

Or maybe most of the writing you do is via email or social media. In that case, keep an eye out for messages or posts that strike you as particularly clear, engaging, and professionally crafted. Then see whether the range and frequency of punctuation in them differ from the range and frequency in your own messages and posts. If a big gap exists, identify at least two steps you can take to close it.

# CHAPTER 11

# Semicolons and Complex Lists

*I feel the need to punctuate my joy*
*With frequent semicolons*
*Of existential anguish*

—Buff Whitman-Bradley, "Semicolons of Anguish" (2013)

The previous chapter highlighted how punctuation affects other punctuation. A good illustration of that involves a secondary application of semicolons. In addition to using them to connect independent clauses or other constructions that can stand alone as sentences, you can also use them to organize complex lists.

By "complex lists," I mean lists in which there is already a comma in one or more of the items. Here's an example given by Patricia O'Conner in *Woe Is I: The Grammarphobe's Guide to Better English in Plain English*:

> Fred's favorite things were his robe, a yellow chenille number from Barneys; his slippers; his overstuffed chair, which had once been his father's; murder mysteries, especially those by Sue Grafton; and single-malt.

In a typical list, commas are sufficient. They clearly separate each individual item. But that's not the case with O'Conner's list because some of the items, like the robe, already have commas built into their descriptions.

When we read "his robe, a yellow chenille number from Barneys," we are not encountering two items separated by a comma. We are encountering only one item—a robe—with some additional information tacked on: the color of the robe (yellow), the material of the robe (chenille), and the store the robe came from (Barneys).

The same is true as we move farther down the list. The "overstuffed chair" and the explanatory phrase "which had once been his father's" should be grouped together as one unit. So should "murder mysteries" and "especially those by Sue Grafton."

If commas were the way to organize all this information, readers would have a much harder time recognizing where one item ended and the next began. We need an additional punctuation mark to help us avoid that kind of confusion.

Enter semicolons. Semicolons helpfully demarcate

- item 1 ("his robe") from item 2 ("his slippers"),
- item 2 ("his slippers") from item 3 ("his overstuffed chair"),
- and so on.

Consider, for example, the following sentence from Volume 1 of *The History of the Decline and Fall of the Roman Empire* by the 18th-century British historian Edward Gibbon. Here's what it would look like without semicolons:

> They took up arms with savage fierceness, they laid them down, or turned them against each other, with wild inconsistency, and while they fought singly, they were successfully subdued.

Now read the same sentence again— but this time with the separating semicolons that were helpfully included by Gibbon, whose style has been admired by writers as different as Thomas Jefferson, Winston Churchill, and Isaac Asimov:

Edward Gibbon

> They took up arms with savage fierceness; they laid them down, or turned them against each other, with wild inconsistency; and while they fought singly, they were successfully subdued.

Notice that Gibbon also adds the first kind of semicolon we learned about, the one that connects independent clauses. If we separate the units into a list of three, we can see that each can stand alone as its own sentence:

- "They took up arms with savage fierceness."
- "They laid them down, or turned them against each other, with wild inconsistency."
- "While they fought singly, they were successively subdued."

It's like a mini-lesson on semicolons neatly wrapped in one compact classical construction.

\* \* \*

To demonstrate that this sort of structure appears in more recent writing as well, take a look at how former Supreme Court justice Anthony Kennedy uses semicolons, over two hundred years after Gibbon, in *State Farm v. Campbell*, a landmark case about limits on punitive damages:

> The harm arose from a transaction in the economic realm, not from some physical assault or trauma; there were no physical injuries; and State Farm paid the excess verdict before the complaint was filed, so the Campbells suffered only minor economic injuries for the 18-month period in which State Farm refused to resolve the claim against them.

Like Gibbon, Kennedy packs essentially three sentences into one thanks to the strategic placement of semicolons. As a result, he makes a complex bundle of information a lot easier to track and absorb.

Justice Anthony Kennedy

**Additional Advice**

1. "When items in series themselves contain commas, additional punctuation is needed to clarify the items. Consider this sentence:

   The invited speakers are the association's president, the vice president, the councilwoman, Suzette Tanner, and Walter McCarthy, the executive director.

   Here, commas aren't enough to clarify the items in the series: is the councilwoman named Suzette Tanner or are Suzette Tanner and the councilwoman two people? Adding serial semicolons provides clarity:

   The invited speakers are the association's president; the vice president; the councilwoman, Suzette Tanner; and Walter McCarthy, the executive director.

   The semicolons make it clear that there are four speakers."
   —Erika Suffern, "Serial Commas and
   Serial Semicolons" (2017)

2. "The commas between items can be 'bumped up' a notch and turned into semicolons, so that readers can easily tell how many items are in the list and which words go together: *I bought shiny, ripe apples; small, sweet, juicy grapes; and firm pears.*"
   —University of North Carolina at Chapel Hill Writing
   Center "Semicolons, Colons, and Dashes" (2021)

3. "With educated people, I suppose, punctuation is a matter of rule; with me it is a matter of feeling. But I must say that I have a great respect for the semicolon; it's a very useful little chap."

—Abraham Lincoln, quoted by Wayne C. Temple in
*Lincoln's Confidant: The Life of Noah Brooks* (1864)

**Punctuation Practice: Complex Lists**

1. This chapter focused on how semicolons can be used to organize complex lists. By "complex lists," we mean?

    A. a list that contains a comma splice

    B. a list that contains internal commas

    C. a list that contains internal quotation marks

    D. a list that contains both commas and quotation marks

2. Below is a modified version of what is written on the back flap of Lauren Groff's award-winning novel *Fates and Furies*, where an author's biography often appears. I say "modified version" because I've removed the semicolons and switched them to commas. Try to put the appropriate semicolons back in:

    Lauren Groff is the *New York Times* bestselling author of two novels, *The Monsters of Templeton* and *Arcadia*, as well as the story collection *Delicate Edible Birds*. Her work has been featured in the *New Yorker*, *Harper's*, *The Atlantic*, and several *Best American Short Stories* series, has won the Paul Bowles Prize for Fiction, the PEN/O. Henry Award, the Pushcart Prize, and has been a finalist for the Orange Award for New Writers and a finalist for the *Los Angeles Times* Book Prize.

**Answers Explained**

1. The correct answer is **B**. A "complex list" is a list that contains internal commas. The first example in this chapter was from Patricia O'Conner's book *Woe Is I*:

> Fred's favorite things were his robe, a yellow chenille number from Barneys; his slippers; his overstuffed chair, which had once been his father's; murder mysteries, especially those by Sue Grafton; and single-malt.

Had O'Connor not included semicolons and instead just gone with commas, her list would be a real headache to navigate:

> Fred's favorite things were his robe, a yellow chenille number from Barneys, his slippers, his overstuffed chair, which had once been his father's, murder mysteries, especially those by Sue Grafton, and single-malt.

2. "Lauren Groff is the *New York Times* bestselling author of two novels, *The Monsters of Templeton* and *Arcadia*, as well as the story collection *Delicate Edible Birds*. Her work has been featured in the *New Yorker*, *Harper's*, *The Atlantic*, and several *Best American Short Stories* series; has won the Paul Bowles Prize for Fiction, the PEN/O. Henry Award, the Pushcart Prize; and has been a finalist for the Orange Award for New Writers and a finalist for the *Los Angeles Times* Book Prize."

# CHAPTER 12

# Semicolon Deviation

*I use a whole lot of half-assed semicolons;
there was one of them just now; that
was a semicolon after "semicolons,"
and another one after "now."*

—Ursula K. Le Guin, *The Wave in the Mind: Talks and Essays
on the Writer, the Reader, and the Imagination* (2004)

We've now learned that semicolons have two functions:

- They can connect independent clauses and other constructions that can stand alone as a sentence.
- They can help organize complex lists.

So then what explains the following passage from Andy Weir in his best-selling book *The Martian*? (The book was so successful that it was eventually turned into a movie starring Matt Damon.)

> Everyone on the mission had two specialties. I'm a botanist and mechanical engineer; basically, the mission's fix-it man who played with plants.

Or what about this next sentence by the journalist Frank O'Brien? It appears in an article called "The Unknown Soldier" that earned O'Brien the 1922 Pulitzer Prize for Editorial Writing:

> This man who died for his country is the symbol of these qualities; a far more perfect symbol than any man could be whose name and deeds we knew.

Are these semicolons accidents? Are they errant punctuation marks that somehow slipped by each author and their editors?

Probably not. More likely, they're stylistic choices. Maybe Andy Weir wanted to create an extra delay between the first part of his sentence ("I'm a botanist and mechanical engineer") and its playfully explanatory ending ("basically, the mission's fix-it man who played with plants"). Maybe Frank O'Brien wanted something similar, although in the service of a much more somber end.

Whatever each author's motivation, these deviations are another helpful reminder that the line between grammatical deviance and grammatical diversity isn't always easy to pinpoint. As the journalist Dante Ramos explained in a column for the *Boston Globe* back in

2016, "Punctuation rules aren't measures of our moral worth; they're adaptations to the mood and the machinery of their times."

At some point, maybe the professional world will shift back to a situation where semicolons are more liberally used. But if you are at all nervous about the impression your writing will make, I recommend sticking to the more conventional function of semicolons, at least for now. That's what Ramos himself did, both in the sentence we just read and also in the sentence right after it in his column:

> Likewise, millennials who omit periods at the end of text messages aren't being lazy or incoherent; they're recognizing the limits of the technology at hand.

Two independent clauses. Two related ideas. Together, they create one strong reason to opt for a semicolon in its standard form.

## Additional Advice

1. "The rules of punctuation that are useful for ordinary cases are wisely broken in special emergencies."

   —E. L. Thorndike, "The Psychology of Punctuation" (1948)

2. "This law of non-dominance also governs the weakest type of semicolon, which Mr. Nunberg calls a 'promotion semicolon,' a semicolon that would have been a comma if there were not already too many commas in the sentence. Here is an example: 'he has written books on Tinker, the shortstop; Evans the second baseman; and Chance, the first baseman. In this sentence all semicolons are created equal, and they are all more equal than the commas."

   —Sarah Boxer, "If Not Strong, At Least Tricky: The Middleweight of Punctuation Politics" (1999)

3. "The things I like best in T. S. Eliot's poetry, especially in the *Four Quartets*, are the semicolons. You cannot hear them, but they are there, laying out the connections between the images and the ideas. Sometimes you get a glimpse of a semicolon coming, a few lines farther on, and it is like climbing a steep path through woods and seeing a wooden bench just at a bend in the road ahead, a place where you can expect to sit for a moment, catching your breath."

   —Lewis Thomas, *The Medusa and the Snail: More Notes of a Biology Watcher* (1979)

**Punctuation Practice: Style and Semicolons**

Which of the examples below deviate from current conventions about how to use semicolons like a professional, at least in the United States?* Mark all that apply:

A. "Charles wanted the child to be called after her mother; Emma opposed this."

—Gustave Flaubert, *Madame Bovary* (1856)

B. "But the matter is not really one of aesthetics; not here."

—Julian Barnes, *Flaubert's Parrot* (1984)

C. "Writing is finally a series of permissions you give yourself to be expressive in certain ways. To invent. To leap. To fly. To fall. To find your own characteristic way of narrating and insisting; that is, to find your own inner freedom."

—Susan Sontag, *Where the Stress Falls* (2001)

D. "This way of leaving your family for work had condemned them over several generations to have their hearts always in other places, their minds thinking about people elsewhere; they could never be in a single existence at one time. How wonderful it was going to be to have things otherwise."

—Kiran Desai, *The Inheritance of Loss* (2006)

---

* Punctuation conventions in Britain and other English-speaking areas can sometimes conflict. For a quick breakdown of the differences, check out "British versus American Style" on the website of the Punctuation Guide (https://www.thepunctuationguide.com/british-versus-american-style.html).

**Answers Explained**

The passage from Julian Barnes (B) and the passage from Susan Sontag (C) both deviate from current conventions about how to use a semicolon in the United States. Neither uses a semicolon either to connect independent clauses (Chapter 9) or to organize a complex list (Chapter 11).

# CHAPTER 13

# Dependent Clauses

*[Marcel] Proust takes particular delight in dependent clauses, because they illustrate the dependence of man upon chance, of the individual upon the whole.*

—Leo Spitzer, "Zum Stil Marcel Proust's" (1961)

In the last few chapters, we've talked about the semicolon—that sometimes intimidating, even polarizing, hybrid between a comma and a period. The unease this punctuation mark creates in many people is nicely captured by Richard Wydick in *Plain English for Lawyers* through an analogy to wild mushrooms. "Some are delicious but others are deadly," he imagines people thinking of both mushrooms and semicolons, "and since it is hard to tell the difference, they should all be avoided."

My hope is that even if you remain wary of semicolons in general, you'll at least be able to identify the delicious ones from the deadly ones. Key to that ability is learning how to spot independent clauses and dependent clauses, given that it is typically only independent clauses that semicolons connect.

We've gone over independent clauses in previous chapters. But we haven't spent much time on dependent clauses yet, so let's begin to learn about them now. We'll start with the clause part of the term.

Here's how the *Oxford English Dictionary* (*OED*) defines a clause in its glossary of grammatical terms:

> A clause is a grammatical unit which typically contains a verb (or verb phrase), and which may be a complete sentence in itself or may form part of a sentence.

There is a lot going on in that definition. But the important thing to focus on is that a clause contains a verb. For example, when Abraham Lincoln begins the Gettysburg Address with the words "Four score and seven years ago," he hasn't yet created a clause. He has created a *phrase*, which the *OED* places somewhere "between a word and a clause" and says usually "function[s] in the same way as a word on its own." But because there is no verb in "Four score and seven years ago," it likely won't be considered a clause.

As for the difference between independent clauses and dependent clauses, the distinguishing characteristics are built into each name.

An independent clause is a clause that can exist on its own as a sentence: it's "independent."

Think of it as a fully functioning adult. It doesn't need rent money. It doesn't need you to do its laundry, iron its clothes, or pay its credit card bill. It can completely support itself, without any extra help. Here's an example from *Brown v. Board of Education*, the landmark US Supreme Court case that ruled that racial segregation in public schools is unconstitutional: "Separate educational facilities are inherently unequal."

A dependent clause, on the other hand, needs a lot of extra help. It's not a fully functioning adult. Instead, it very much "depends" on outside support. In particular, it depends on an independent clause, at least if the goal is to form a sentence. It's not capable of creating one on its own.

Consider a piece of editing advice offered by the legendary crime novelist Elmore Leonard: "If it sounds like writing, I rewrite it." The first clause in that statement ("If it sounds like writing") can't stand alone as a sentence. It depends on the second clause ("I rewrite it"). So we call that first clause a *dependent clause*.

This distinction between independent clauses and dependent clauses will become even more important in the next chapter when we take a closer look at the punctuation mark that always seems to give my students the most trouble: the comma.

**Additional Advice**

1. "A dependent clause cannot stand on its own. It needs an independent clause to complete a sentence. Dependent clauses often begin with *although, since, if, when,* and *because.*"

   —Yale Center for Teaching and Learning,
   "Types of Clauses" (2015)

2. "A 'dependent marker' word is a word added to the beginning of an independent clause that makes it into a dependent clause.

   <u>When</u> Jim studied in the Sweet Shop for his chemistry quiz, it was very noisy.

   Some common dependent markers are: *after, although, as, as if, because, before, even if, even though, if, in order to, since, though, unless, until, whatever, when, whenever, whether,* and *while.*"

   —Purdue Online Writing Lab, "Identifying
   Independent and Dependent Clauses" (2021)

3. "The adverb clause, the most common type of dependent clause, serves a variety of purposes in the sentence. Some of its most common functions are to indicate time and place, to provide reasons and explanations, and to describe methods, conditions, and outcomes. The adverb clause begins with a subordinating conjunction.

   Common subordinating conjunctions: *as, after, although, because, even though, if, now that, provided, rather than, since, unless, until, when, whereas, whether,* and *while.*

If an adverb clause occurs before an independent clause, it is followed by a comma:

Example: Because traffic was so heavy, I was late.

If an adverb clause occurs after an independent clause, it is NOT preceded by a comma unless it begins with *although*, *whereas*, or some other term that indicates contrast.

Example: I was late because traffic was so heavy.

Example: I was late, although traffic was relatively light for the time of day."

—University of Texas at Dallas Writing Center,
"Commas and Dependent Clauses" (2021)

**Punctuation Practice: Clause Clarification**

Which of the following sentences contain at least one dependent clause? Mark all that apply:

A. "When there is no place for the scalpel, words are the surgeon's only tools."

—Paul Kalanithi, *When Breath Becomes Air* (2016)

B. "A word after a word after a word is power."

—Margaret Atwood, "Spelling" (1981)

C. "If I was going to have a better life, I was going to have to write it."

—Ann Patchett, *The Getaway Car* (2011)

D. "I started writing because I had a need inside me to create something that was not there."

—Audre Lorde, *A Litany for Survival* (1995)

### Answers Explained

**A. Contains a Dependent Clause:** The sentence from Paul Kalanithi's *When Breath Becomes Air* contains a dependent clause: "When there is no place for the scalpel." That clause has a subject and a verb, but it is not a complete thought. It can't stand alone as a sentence but rather *depends* on the independent clause in the sentence ("words are the surgeon's only tools").

**B. Does Not Contain a Dependent Clause:** The sentence from Margaret Atwood's "Spelling" does <u>not</u> include a dependent clause. The only clause it contains is an independent clause.

**C. Contains a Dependent Clause:** The sentence from Ann Patchett's *The Getaway Car* contains a dependent clause: "If I was going to have." Like the dependent clause in the Paul Kalanithi sentence in choice A, this clause has a subject and a verb, but it is not a complete thought.

**D. Contains a Dependent Clause:** The sentence from Audre Lorde contains a dependent clause: "because I had a need inside me to create something that was not there." Like the dependent clauses in the Paul Kalanithi sentence and the Ann Patchett sentence, this clause has a subject and a verb, but it is not a complete thought. The reason there is no comma in the sentence is that this dependent clause comes after—not before—the independent clause. We'll learn more about that distinction in the next chapter, with the help of the 20th-century dancer Isadora Duncan.

# CHAPTER 14

# Isadora Duncan

*I had learned the methodical persistence of the researcher who checks even the commas.*

—Elena Ferrante, *The Story of a New Name* (2012)

There is a fun story about commas that sometimes involves the French writer Gustave Flaubert and sometimes involves the Irish writer Oscar Wilde. It probably isn't true of both of them. It may not even be true of either of them. But the punch line—"I spent the morning taking out a comma, and the afternoon putting one back in"—illustrates a couple of helpful points:

Gustave Flaubert

• Great writers tend to think carefully about the placement of even a single punctuation mark.
• Commas in particular can cause people to question whether using one is appropriate.

Oscar Wilde

Previous chapters have covered how to think about commas when you are connecting an independent clause with another independent clause. But what about when you are connecting an independent clause with a dependent clause?

For that, we can get some help from a dancer named Isadora Duncan, who was born in San Francisco in the late 1870s but spent much of her professional career performing in Western Europe and what was then called the Soviet Union.

Isadora Duncan

I remember learning about Duncan in middle school. Two things stand out. The first is the way she died. On September 14, 1927, she was driving a fancy French convertible when the silk scarf she was wearing got caught in one of the spokes of the wheels and broke her neck.

The second is that the person who told me this gruesomely vivid story said it could help me figure out how to punctuate sentences that contain an independent clause and a dependent clause.

Think, for example, of the way that Isadora Duncan's name might be written on an attendance sheet or class roster. It would be "Isadora Duncan" (without a comma) if the roster started with first names. Or it would be "Duncan, Isadora" (with a comma) if it started with last names. Now remove all the letters except for "I" and "D." Finally, match "I" and "D" with the types of clauses those letters signify:

- **I**ndependent **D**ependent
- **D**ependent, **I**ndependent

When you put an independent clause before a dependent clause—when you put "**I**sadora" before "**D**uncan"—you generally don't need a comma. But when you put a dependent clause before an independent clause—when you put "**D**uncan" before "**I**sadora"—you generally *do* need a comma.

Here's an example from Duncan's autobiography, *My Life*. She's describing the formal education she received and how she found it to be unhelpfully restrictive: "When I could escape from the prison of school, I was free." That sentence gets a comma because a dependent clause ("When I could escape from the prison of school") comes before an independent clause ("I was free"). It's "**D**uncan, **I**sadora."

But if the sentence were written in reverse, the comma wouldn't be necessary: "I was free when I could escape from the prison of school." That's not a dependent clause followed by an independent clause. That's not "**Duncan**, Isadora." That's "Isadora **Duncan**." No comma.

* * *

I realize that this Isadora Duncan approach to commas is a rather macabre, roundabout way to learn about punctuation. That said, I'm pretty sure I only heard it once back when I was a kid, and I have remembered it ever since. Plus, when I tell it to students, the lesson sticks in a way that other approaches don't.

Of course, if you'd like a less morbid memory cue, focus on someone you know whose initials are "I" and "D." Maybe you grew up with a guy named "**I**an **D**uncan." Maybe your aunt's name is "**I**rene **D**ouglass." Whatever your mental marker, the "I before D, D before I" distinction should help you sort out a good deal of comma decisions. In the next and final chapter, we'll cover a few more.

**Additional Advice**

1. "Commas can help create the rhythm of a sentence."
   —Sol Stein, *Sol Stein's Reference Book for Writers* (2010)

2. "Popping in a comma can be like slipping on the necklace that gives an outfit quiet elegance, or like catching the sound of running water that complements, as it completes, the silence of a Japanese landscape."
   —Pico Iyer, "In Praise of the Humble Comma" (2001)

3. "April 6—Today, I learned, the comma, this is, a, comma (,) a period, with, a tail, Miss Kinnian, says its, important, because, it makes writing, better, she said, somebody, could lose, a lot, of money, if a comma, isn't in, the right, place, I got, some money, that I, saved from, my job, and what, the foundation, pays me, but not, much and, I don't see how, a comma, keeps, you from, losing it,

   But, she says, everybody, uses commas, so I'll, use them, too,,,,,,,"
   —Daniel Keyes, *Flowers for Algernon* (1966)

## Punctuation Practice: Isadora Duncan → Duncan, Isadora

### 1. True or False

The following sentence from Salman Rushdie's novel *The Ground Beneath Her Feet* is an example of the "**I**sadora **D**uncan" structure mentioned in this chapter:

Whenever someone who knows you disappears, you lose one version of yourself.

In other words, it is an "**I**ndependent **C**lause" followed by a "**D**ependent **C**lause."*

### 2. Multiple Choice

Which of the following bits of writing advice contain at least one example of the "**D**uncan, **I**sadora" structure that involves having a "**D**ependent **C**lause" precede an "**I**ndependent **C**lause"? Mark all that apply:

A. "Leave a decent space of time between writing something and editing it."
   —Zadie Smith, "Zadie Smith's Rules for Writers" (2010)

B. "Omit needless words."
   —William Strunk Jr. and E. B. White,
   *The Elements of Style* (1959)

---

* I have capitalized and bolded "**I**ndependent **C**lause" and "**D**ependent **C**lause" in this section to help you better visualize the way those terms map onto "**I**sadora **D**uncan" and "**D**uncan, **I**sadora." Typically, however, the terms are lowercased.

C. "Remember, when people tell you something is wrong or it doesn't work for them, they are almost always right. When they tell you exactly what they think is wrong and how to fix it, they are almost always wrong."

—Neil Gaiman, "For All the People Who
Ask Me for Writing Advice" (2012)

## Answers Explained

1. *True or False*

   **False.** Rushdie's sentence is an example of the opposite structure: "**D**uncan, Isadora." The **D**ependent Clause* ("Whenever someone who knows you disappears") comes before the Independent Clause ("you lose yourself").

2. *Multiple Choice*

   **A. Incorrect.** There is no **D**ependent Clause in the advice from Zadie Smith. There is just an Independent Clause: "Leave a decent space of time between writing something and editing it." So it is "Isadora" without a "**D**uncan."

   **B. Incorrect.** There is no **D**ependent Clause in the advice from William Strunk Jr. and E. B. White. There is just an Independent Clause: "Omit needless words." So it is "Isadora" without a "**D**uncan."

   **C. Correct!** Neil Gaiman's advice contains two examples of a **D**ependent Clause followed by an Independent Clause. The first one is: "when people tell you something is wrong or it doesn't work for them, they are almost always right." The second one is: "When they tell you exactly what they think is wrong and how to fix it, they are almost always wrong." Both are essentially "**D**uncan, Isadora."

# CHAPTER 15

# If-Then

*There is truth and falsehood in the comma.*

—Tom Stoppard, *The Invention of Love* (1997)

An additional example might help solidify the distinction between "Isadora Duncan" and "Duncan, Isadora." It involves a little math—or at least a kind of statement that often appears in mathematical proofs. I am talking about "If-then" statements.

Consider the following passage from *The Calculus of Friendship* by the Cornell mathematician Steven Strogatz. He is sharing what he found so appealing about math when he was an undergraduate at MIT:

> It had justice built into it. If you started right and worked hard and did everything correctly, it might be a slog but you were assured by logic to win in the end.

Notice the implied "If-then" statement:

> It had justice built into it. <u>If</u> you started right and worked hard and did everything correctly, [<u>then</u>] it might be a slog but you were assured by logic to win in the end.

When you write an "If-then" statement, you typically need a comma, like you would when you have a dependent clause before an independent clause. (Think "Duncan, Isadora.") But when the structure reverses, you have more discretion to leave out the comma. For example, Strogatz could have written the sentence in the following way:

> It might be a slog but you were assured by logic to win in the end if you started right and worked hard and did everything correctly.

There are a couple of funky things going on in that revision, including the omission of a comma before "but" and the use of polysyndeton, which involves adding an extra conjunction ("and") for rhetorical effect. So perhaps an example from later in *The Calculus of Friendship* would be more helpful. In it, Strogatz recalls a playful problem his beloved high school calculus teacher, Don Joffray, posed in class one day:

Suppose you put 100 strands of spaghetti into a pot. If you tie the strands together at random until no loose ends remain, what's the total number of loops you expect to form?

When the "If" comes before the "(implied) then," we need a comma: "If you tie the strands together at random until no loose ends remain, what's the total number of loops you expect to form?" But when the "(implied) then" comes before the "If," we're freer to decide whether the comma is helpful or distracting. Which means Strogatz could have very easily rearranged the second sentence in the following way:

Suppose you put 100 strands of spaghetti into a pot. What's the total number of loops you expect to form if you tie the strands together at random until no loose ends remain?

Here's how the *Cambridge Dictionary* explains the difference, using the technical term for the "If" part of an "If-then" statement: conditional clauses.

Conditional clauses usually come before main clauses, but they may also come after them:

- <u>If you see Dora</u>, *will you give her a message?* (conditional clause first; a comma is normally used in writing)
- *I'll go to Bristol tomorrow* <u>if the weather is good</u>. (conditional clause second; a comma is not normally used in writing)

Understanding this relationship between "If" and "then" should make it easier for you to navigate the relationship between independent clauses and dependent clauses, given that a conditional clause is structurally equivalent to a dependent clause. It can't stand alone as a sentence.

Consider even asking yourself the following question when you write or edit something that contains a dependent clause and an independent clause: Which of these clauses seems more like the "If" part of an "If-then" statement, and which seems more like the "then" part?

Suppose, for instance, that you had crafted a sentence that appears in another one of Strogatz's books, *The Joy of X*. It describes the lack of respect given the quadratic formula:

> When mathematicians and physicists are asked to list the top ten most beautiful or important equations of all time, the quadratic formula never makes the cut.

See how the clause that begins with "When" ("<u>When</u> mathematicians and physicists are asked to list the top ten most beautiful or important equations of all time") functions sort of like the "If" part of an "If-then" statement? And see how the clause that begins with "the quadratic" ("<u>the quadratic</u> formula never makes the cut") functions sort of like the "then" part?

Once you recognize that similarity, you might more clearly see why the comma is appropriate. There is an "If" before a "then"—or more accurately, there is a dependent clause before an independent clause.

This kind of reframing won't always account for the different varieties of dependent and independent clauses you can construct. But if it helps you insert commas more skillfully and more confidently, certainly feel free to try it as a starting point.

## Additional Advice

1. "Conditional sentences are usually made up of two parts, a conditional clause and a main clause. The conditional clause is the 'if' part of the sentence and the main clause is the result, what happens. . . . The two clauses can come in any order. In written English, if the conditional clause comes first, you put a comma between it and the main clause. You don't use a comma if the main clause comes first."

   —BBC Grammar Challenge, "Zero Conditional" (2021)

2. "'If-then' statements require commas to separate the two clauses that result: *If* I use correct punctuation, *then* I will include commas where necessary. . . . Even when the statement drops the word *then*, a comma must be used."

   —Constant Content, "If, Then Statements Require Commas" (2007)

3. "When readability would be improved by omitting 'then,' the sentence should instead start with 'When' or 'For,' as in this sentence itself. A comma still follows the condition introduced by 'When' or 'For.' The structure of a sentence beginning with 'Since' is like those beginning with 'When' or 'For'; a comma follows the first clause. After 'Since' or 'Because', the concluding clause *cannot* begin with 'then' or 'so'; 'then' is used only with 'If.'"

   —Douglas B. West, "The Grammar according to West" (2021)

## Punctuation Practice: Commas and Computers

1. Douglas Hofstadter is a professor of cognitive science and computer science at the University of Indiana. His book *Gödel, Escher, Bach* won the Pulitzer Prize for General Nonfiction in 1980. A sentence from it appears below:

   <u>If it weren't for this fact,</u> you could write anything as the first line of a fantasy, and then lift it out into the real world as a theorem.

   The underlined portion of the sentence is

   A. an independent clause
   B. a dependent clause

2. The following sentence is taken from *Hidden Figures: The American Dream and the Untold Story of the Black Women Mathematicians Who Helped Win the Space Race.** The author, Margot Lee Shetterly, is explaining how passionate she became about tracking down these mathematicians, who were often referred to as human "computers":

   My investigation became more like an obsession; I would walk any trail if it meant finding a trace of one of the computers at its end.

   There is no comma before "if" in Shetterly's sentence because

   _____.

   A. the clause that starts with "if" is an independent clause, and when an independent clause follows a dependent clause, you don't need to include a comma

---

\* *Hidden Figures* was turned into a Hollywood movie in 2016.

B. the clause that starts with "if" is a dependent clause, and when a dependent clause follows an independent clause, you don't necessarily need to include a comma

## Answers Explained

1. **B.** We learned in this chapter that the "If" part of an "If-then" statement is a dependent clause. It can't stand alone as a sentence.
2. **B.** We learned in this chapter that when a dependent clause follows an independent clause, you generally don't need to include a comma.

# Epilogue

*That's all we have, finally, the words, and they had better be the right ones, with punctuation in the right places so that they can best say what they are meant to say.*

—Raymond Carver, "A Storyteller's Shoptalk" (1981)

Like math, punctuation can initially seem like it is filled with unfamiliar symbols and relationships. As you learn the underlying patterns and principles, however, the interconnectedness of the whole system becomes much more comprehensible, even beautiful.

My hope is that at least some of that beauty resonated with you while you were reading this book. Commas, semicolons, periods—in the right hands, these small marks of meaning and direction can do some pretty amazing things, as can several kinds of punctuation we haven't covered, including dashes, colons, and parentheses. The plan is to address those in a future volume.

But even if this book is the last punctuation guide you ever read, you've certainly taken an important step toward improving the way you construct sentences and communicate your ideas. Punctuation doesn't have to be a pain point. You need not approach it with anxiety, confusion, or dread. With a little knowledge and a lot of practice, you can instead use it to do more than just sound professional. You can use it to become much more persuasive.

# THANK-YOUS

*A cloud of books floated through the thickened air. There were some loose letters, too, and even some punctuation. They swirled and slowly settled around him. He shook the orb again and held it to his face. A semicolon landed on the desk in front of him. A period landed at his feet.*

—Ruth Ozeki, *The Book of Form and Emptiness* (2021)

There are over 1,500 commas in this book. There are also more than 600 colons, close to 85 semicolons, and nearly 160 dashes. I am very grateful to the people who reviewed every one of them: Sandra Abbo, Hilary Allen, Allie Brydell, Matthew Ender-Silberman, Olivia Field, Gabriela Hindera, Danish Hyder, and Peg Schriener.

I also want to thank Tamar Alexanian, Ravinder Arneja, Jonathan Blaha, Liz Brennan, Will Case, Jonathan Concepcion, Thomas Frashier, James Hager, Wooyoung Lee, Raymond Levine, Zachary Suggs, and Jessica Trafimow. Each of them provided helpful edits on multiple chapters.

As for the team at Maize Books, I am excited that it now includes Carl Lavigne and Marissa Mercurio. Together with Jason Colman, Sean Guynes, and Amanda Karby, they've created a wonderfully efficient and innovative publishing process. I'm glad we get to keep working together.

# NOTES

## Epigraph

vi  "If you aren't interested in punctuation": Ursula K. Le Guin, Steering the Craft: A Twenty-First Century Guide to Sailing the Sea of Story 11 (First Mariner Books ed., The Eighth Mountain Press 2015) (1998).

## Introduction

1  "push-and-pull between personal style and other people's expectations": Cecelia Watson, *How Do You Text? Unpacking the Battle between "Raindrop" and "Waterfall" Texters*, NBC News Think (Sept. 22, 2019, 2:47 P.M.), https://www.nbcnews.com/think/opinion/how-do-you-text-unpacking-battle-between-raindrop-waterfall-texters-ncna1057411.

4  "if the writing is bad": Chief Justice John G. Roberts Jr., *Interviews with United States Supreme Court Justices*, Scribes J. Legal Writing 6 (Bryan Garner ed., 2010).

## Chapter 1: Comma Splices

5  "The comma splice is unnecessary": Robert Lane Greene, *The Dreaded Comma Splice*, Economist (Jan. 10, 2012), https://www.economist.com/johnson/2012/01/10/the-dreaded-comma-splice.

6  "road signs": Pico Iyer, *In Praise of the Humble Comma*, Time (June 24, 2001), http://content.time.com/time/magazine/article/0,9171,149453,00.html.

7　**"slow things down too much"**: Ben Yagoda, How to Not Write Bad: The Most Common Writing Problems and the Best Ways to Avoid Them 51 (2013).

7　**"She was fire, he was ice"**: Trevor Noah, Born a Crime: Stories from a South African Childhood 93 (2016).

7　**"Avon"**: Beauty Is the Journey, Empowerment Is the Destination (illustration), *in Avon Announces Beauty for a Purpose New Brand Statement Reflecting Commitment to Empowering Women*, PR Newswire (June 15, 2015), http://www.multivu.com/players/English/7546151-avon-beauty-for-a -purpose/.

8　**"may be used deliberately"**: Richard Nordquist, *Comma Splices*, ThoughtCo. (Jan. 8, 2020), https://www.thoughtco.com/what-is -comma-splice-1689897.

8　**"You can correct a comma splice in four ways"**: Leslie Perelman, James Paradis & Edward Barrett, The Mayfield Handbook of Technical and Scientific Writing 6.5 (1997) (e-book).

8　**"Even Strunk and White"**: Russell Harper, *Comma Splices and Run-On Sentences*, CMOS Shop Talk (Apr. 16, 2019), https://cmosshoptalk.com/ 2019/04/16/comma-splices-and-run-on-sentences/ (ellipses in original).

10　**"They shoot the white girl first"**: Toni Morrison, Paradise 3 (Vintage International ed., Vintage Books 2014) (1997).

10　**"It was the best of times"**: Charles Dickens, A Tale of Two Cities 3 (James Nisbet & Co. 1902) (1859).

10　**"Three men"**: G. K. Chesterton, *The Crime of the Communist*, *in* The Scandal of Father Brown 99 (Walking Lion Press 2006) (1935).

10　**"born twice"**: Jeffrey Eugenides, Middlesex 3 (2002).

10　**"We are united"**: Lydia Davis, Can't and Won't: Stories 144 (Macmillan 2014).

## Chapter 2: "However"

13　**"perceived as a mistake"**: *However*, Am. Heritage Dictionary, https:// ahdictionary.com/word/search.html?q=however (last visited Feb. 5, 2021).

14　**"We have not ended racial caste"**: Michelle Alexander, The New Jim Crow: Mass Incarceration in the Age of Colorblindness 2 (2012).

14　**"It's our signature"**: *Our Menus*, Ruth's Chris Steak House, https:// ruthschris.net/our-menus/ (last visited May 1, 2021) (emphasis added).

14 **"It's a Residence"**: AngeloMazzamuto, *Marriott Residence Inn "It's Not a Room Elephant,"* YouTube (June 13, 2012), https://www.youtube.com/watch?v=WBFGfTE6tVQ (emphasis added).

15 **"it tells history"**: Fanaticepl, *Rolex AO 2017 Ad It Doesn't Just Tell Time It Tells History*, YouTube (Jan. 27, 2017), https://www.youtube.com/watch?v=zf0_razdqGs.

15 **"Both stories are selective, neither is false"**: Thomas Grey, *Bad Man from Olympus*, New York Review of Books (July 13, 2015).

16 **"not immutable"**: Rudolf Flesch, The Art of Readable Writing: With the Flesch Readability Formula 94 (1949).

16 **"never stops"**: Daniel Tammet, Every Word Is a Bird We Teach to Sing: Encounters with the Mysteries and Meanings of Language 50 (2012).

16 **"significant trend in that direction"**: Lizzie Hutton & Anne Curzan, *The Grammatical Status of* However, 47 J. Eng. Linguistics 29 (2019).

17 **"judged negatively"**: *Id.* at 48.

17 **"few writers consistently follow this rule"**: *However*, Am. Heritage Dictionary, https://ahdictionary.com/word/search.html?q=however (last visited Feb. 5, 2021).

19 **"The usage of punctuation"**: Mark Nichol, *How to Punctuate with "However,"* Daily Writing Tips, https://www.dailywritingtips.com/how-to-punctuate-with-however/ (last visited May 1, 2021).

19 **"grammarians call it a conjunctive adverb"**: Claire Kehrwald Cook, Line by Line: How to Edit Your Own Writing 28 (1985).

19 **"stylistic suggestion"**: Wayne Schiess, *Beginning with "However"?*, Legal Writing (Feb. 6, 2018), https://sites.utexas.edu/legalwriting/2018/02/06/beginning-with-however/.

20 **"The division of labour"**: Adam Smith, The Wealth of Nations 5 (Modern Library 2000) (1776).

20 **"He clearly saw"**: Charles Darwin, The Origin of Species 12 (P. F. Collier & Son 1909) (1859).

20 **"ray of light"**: Albert Einstein, Relativity: The Special and the General Theory 88 (Robert W. Lawson trans., Henry Holt & Co. 1920) (1916).

## Chapter 3: Adverbial Conjunctions

23 **"Like a few other adverbs"**: Bryan Garner, Garner's Modern English Usage 492 (4th ed. 2016).

24 **"coordinating conjunctions"**: For an argument that the traditional category of "conjunctions" is imprecise and unhelpful, see Steven Pinker, The Sense of Style 88 (2014). He prefers the term *coordinator*.

24 **"melancholy temperament"**: Doris Kearns Goodwin, *Introduction* to Team of Rivals: The Political Genius of Abraham Lincoln xvii (2006).

25 **"Henrietta's cells"**: Rebecca Skloot, The Immortal Life of Henrietta Lacks 57 (2010).

25 **"helpful resource"**: Note, however, that the Wisconsin site uses one of the alternative names for adverbial conjunctions: conjunctive adverbs.

25 **"Adverbial conjunctions"**: *Using Conjunctive Adverbs*, Univ. of Wis. Writing Ctr., https://writing.wisc.edu/handbook/grammarpunct/conjadv/ (last visited May 1, 2021).

26 **"preceded by a semicolon and followed by a comma"**: *Id.*

26 **"any other position"**: *Id.*

26 **"Weekdays revolved on a sameness wheel"**: Maya Angelou, I Know Why the Caged Bird Sings 108 (2002).

29 **"creating intelligent and high-quality content"**: Britainy Sorenson, *How to Use Conjunctive Adverbs*, BKA Content (Dec. 1, 2020), https://www.bkacontent.com/use-conjunctive-adverbs/.

29 **"any part of a sentence"**: *Common Problems with However, Therefore, and Similar Words*, Ind. Univ. of Pa. Writing Ctr., https://www.iup.edu/writingcenter/writing-resources/grammar/common-problems-with-however,-therefore,-and-similar-words/ (last visited May 1, 2021).

29 **"no way related to tropical diseases"**: *Conjunctive Adverbs*, Naval Postgraduate Sch. Grad. Writing Ctr., https://nps.edu/web/gwc/conjunctive-adverbs (last visited May 1, 2021).

30 **"Discipline is something we have to work at"**: Atul Gawande, The Checklist Manifesto: How to Get Things Right 183 (2010).

30 **"Good checklists"**: *Id.* at 120.

31 **"Maybe our idea of heroism"**: *Id.* at 173.

31 **"Knowledge has"**: *Id.* at 13.

## Chapter 4: Coordinating Conjunctions

33   **"we would be Bruce Springsteen and the E Street Band"**: Bruce Springsteen, Born to Run 235–36 (2016).

34   **"hold together grammatically parallel words"**: Constance Hale, Sin and Syntax: How to Craft Wicked Good Prose 123 (2nd ed. 2013).

35   **"Sahara Desert"**: Oliver Sacks, The Man Who Mistook His Wife for a Hat 11 (1998).

35   **"looked aghast"**: *Id.*

37   **"joins two elements of equal grammatical"**: Catherine Traffis, *What Is a Coordinating Conjunction?*, Grammarly: Grammarly Blog (May 18, 2017), https://www.grammarly.com/blog/coordinating-conjunctions/.

37   **"clauses of result or decision"**: *So*, Cambridge Dictionary, https://dictionary.cambridge.org/us/grammar/british-grammar/so (last visited Feb. 9, 2021).

38   **"The *for* clause"**: Edwin Battistella, *Conjunction Dysfunction*, Oxford University Press: OUP Blog (Aug. 4, 2020), https://blog.oup.com/2020/08/conjunction-dysfunction/.

39   **"grammatically equivalent elements"**: William Strunk Jr. & E. B. White, The Elements of Style 5 (1959).

39   **"She looked over her shoulder"**: Gabriel García Márquez, News of a Kidnapping 1 (1996).

## Chapter 5: Coordinating Conjunctions (Deviations)

43   **"always inserting commas"**: Hilton Als, *Toni Morrison and the Ghosts in the House*, New Yorker (Oct. 19, 2003), https://www.newyorker.com/magazine/2003/10/27/ghosts-in-the-house.

44   **"ketchup bottles"**: John Updike, Conversations with John Updike 29 (James Plath ed., 1994).

44   **"funny feeling"**: *See* John Updike, Rabbit Redux 273 (1996).

46   **"Writing is a negotiation"**: John Seabrook, *Can a Machine Learn to Write for the* New Yorker?, New Yorker (Oct. 14, 2019), https://www.newyorker.com/magazine/2019/10/14/can-a-machine-learn-to-write-for-the-new-yorker.

46   **"as few commas as possible"**: Florence King, Reflections in a Jaundiced Eye 107 (1989).

46 **"Rules and informal rules don't exist for their own sake"**: Lawrence Weinstein, Grammar for a Full Life: How the Ways We Shape a Sentence Can Limit or Enlarge Us 27 (2020).

47 **"if a grammar 'rule' is worth following"**: Steven Pinker, *10 "Grammar Rules" It's OK to Break (Sometimes)*, Guardian (Aug. 15, 2014, 8:00 A.M.), https://www.theguardian.com/books/2014/aug/15/steven-pinker-10 -grammar-rules-break.

47 **"more syllabi than any other text"**: *Most Frequently Assigned Titles*, Open Syllabus Explorer, https://opensyllabus.org/ (last visited May 1, 2021).

47 **"Do not join"**: William Strunk Jr., Elements of Style 11–12 (1920).

## Chapter 6: "Language Is Rich, and Malleable"

49 **"changing patterns of literacy"**: M. B. Parks, Pause and Effect: An Introduction to the History of Punctuation in the West 2 (1992).

50 **"Language is rich, and malleable"**: Mary Oliver, A Poetry Handbook 34 (1994).

50 **"with whom I can struggle, and fail"**: Jhumpa Lahiri, In Other Words 27 (Ann Goldstein trans., Vintage Books 2017) (2015).

51 **"graduated magna cum laude from Harvard"**: For a chronicle of the time Cummings spent at Harvard, *see* Christopher Sawyer-Lauçanno, E. E. Cummings: A Biography 43–90 (2004).

52 **"Austen sticking a comma"**: Geoff Nunberg, *Jane Austen: Missing the Points*, UPenn: Language Log (Nov. 17, 2010, 3:50 P.M.), https://languagelog.ldc.upenn.edu/nll/?p=2782.

52 **"I sometimes ignore the rules about commas"**: Mary Norris, Between You & Me: Confessions of a Comma Queen 108 (2015) (quoting James Salter).

52 **"great writers break all the rules of grammar"**: Christian Kiefer, *How Does Garth Greenwell Make Such Wonderful Sentences?*, LitHub (2020), https://lithub.com/how-does-garth-greenwell-make-such-wonderful -sentences/.

53 **"she discovered pot, and sex"**: Nick Paumgarten, *Id Girls*, New Yorker (June 16, 2014), https://www.newyorker.com/magazine/2014/06/23/id -girls.

53   "deeper than ever before, and darker": *Politics and the New Machine*, NEW YORKER (Nov. 8, 2015), https://www.newyorker.com/magazine/2015/11/16/politics-and-the-new-machine.

53   "cured the common cold, or put a man on Pluto": MICHAEL LEWIS, MONEYBALL: THE ART OF WINNING AN UNFAIR GAME 81 (2003).

53   "He was Irish, and illegal": EDWARD DELANEY, *The Drowning*, THE ATLANTIC (Mar. 1, 1994).

## Chapter 7: Conjunctions Affect Other Conjunctions

55   "a sentence that isn't, in fact, correct, but it sings": COLUM MCCANN, LETTERS TO A YOUNG WRITER: SOME PRACTICAL AND PHILOSOPHICAL ADVICE 112 (2017).

56   "with whom I can struggle, and fail": JHUMPA LAHIRI, IN OTHER WORDS 27 (Ann Goldstein trans., Vintage Books 2017) (2015).

56   "Suppose Congress enacted": *Nat'l Fed'n of Indep. Bus. v. Sebelius*, 567 U.S. 519, 569 (2012).

58   "never be scared to reject": HAROLD EVANS, DO I MAKE MYSELF CLEAR? WHY WRITING WELL MATTERS 21 (2017).

59   "Grammar exists": Kristen Csuti, *"Because" Is a Coordinating Conjunction. Fight Me.*, LIT NERDS (Aug. 8, 2019), https://thelitnerds.com/2019/08/08/because-is-a-coordinating-conjunction-fight-me/.

59   "people think of commas purely in terms of right and wrong": Christopher Altman, *Stylistic Commas: To Comma or Not to Comma?*, WRITER'S TOOLBOX (June 4, 2013), https://christopheraltman.wordpress.com/2013/06/04/stylistic-commas-to-comma-or-not-to-comma/.

59   "Your sentences shouldn't leave your reader hyperventilating": Kim Cooper, *Tips on Grammar, Punctuation, and Style*, HARV. COLL. WRITING CTR., https://writingcenter.fas.harvard.edu/pages/tips-grammar-punctuation-and-style.

## Chapter 8: Starting Sentences with "And" or "But"

63   "Everybody agrees": *Is It Ever Okay to Start a Sentence with "And"?*, MERRIAM-WEBSTER DICTIONARY OF ENGLISH USAGE, https://www.merriam-webster.com/words-at-play/words-to-not-begin-sentences-with#:~:text=It's%20perfectly%20acceptable%20to%20begin,school%20children%20from%20stringing%20too.

64 **"Great Nonrules of the English Language"**: Benjamin Dreyer, Dreyer's English: An Utterly Correct Guide to Clarity and Style 7–12 (2019).

64 **"Great writers start sentences with 'And' or 'But' all the time"**: *Id.* at 9.

64 **"a relentless habit"**: *Id.*

64 **"monotonous repetition"**: *Id.* at 9 n.1.

66 **"shocked faces"**: Edwin Battistella, *It's Fine to Start Sentences with "And,"* Oxford University Press: OUP Blog (Feb. 14, 2016), https://blog.oup.com/2016/02/start-sentences-with-and/.

66 **"an empty superstition"**: Kingsley Amis, The King's English: A Guide to Modern Usage 14 (1997).

66 **"And God said"**: *Genesis 1:3*, King James Bible (1611), https://www.kingjamesbibleonline.org/Genesis-1-3/.

67 **"AP Stylebook rule"**: Ted Kitterman, *Why You Should Stop Starting Sentences with "And" or "But,"* Ragan's PR Daily (Jan. 7, 2019), https://www.prdaily.com/why-you-should-stop-starting-sentences-with-and-or-but/#:~:text=There's%20no%20AP%20Stylebook%20rule,But%20don't%20overuse%20it.&text=Many%20translations%20of%20the%20Bible,%E2%80%94and%20prescriptive%E2%80%94usage%20guides.

## Chapter 9: Be Kind to Semicolons

69 **"The semicolon was born"**: Cecelia Watson, *The Birth of the Semicolon,* The Paris Review (Aug. 1, 2019).

70 **"Dorothea quite"**: George Eliot, Middlemarch: A Study of Provincial Life 10 (1876).

71 **"show you've been to college"**: Kurt Vonnegut, A Man without a Country 23 (2007).

71 **"upper-crust"**: Mary Norris, Between You & Me: Confessions of a Comma Queen 140 (2015).

71 **"semicolon virtuoso"**: Ben Yagoda, The Sound on the Page 68 (2004).

72 **"Be kind to the semicolon"**: *In Praise of the Semicolon,* Princeton Writes (Oct. 31, 2013), https://pwrites.princeton.edu/2013/10/31/in-praise-of-the-semicolon/.

73 **"Used well"**: Mary Norris, Between You & Me: Confessions of a Comma Queen 142 (2015).

73 **"William James's paragraphs"**: Ben Dolnick, *Semicolons: A Love Story*, N.Y. Times (July 2, 2012, 9:30 P.M.), https://opinionator.blogs.nytimes .com/2012/07/02/semicolons-a-love-story/.

73 **"a long comma, or a wimpy period"**: Merrill Perlman, *To Semicolon, or Not to Semicolon*, Colum. Journalism Rev. (Apr. 20, 2015), https:// www.cjr.org/analysis/how_to_use_semicolons.php#:~:text=Associated %20Press%20style%20has%20called,be%20connected%20in%20separate %20sentences.

## Chapter 10: Punctuation Affects Other Punctuation

77 **"can take the pressure off"**: Noah Lukeman, A Dash of Style 37 (2006).

78 **"a mountaineer's cleat"**: Karl Ove Knausgaard, My Struggle: Book i 331 (2009).

80 **"Overuse of any punctuation mark"**: Philip Cowell, *What Overusing Exclamation Marks Says about You*, BBC (Mar. 2, 2017), https://www.bbc .com/culture/article/20170301-what-overusing-exclamation-marks-says -about-you.

80 **"the risks of missteps"**: Philip B. Corbett, *Dashes Everywhere*, N.Y. Times: After Deadline (Apr. 5, 2011), https://afterdeadline.blogs.nytimes .com/2011/04/05/dashes-everywhere/.

80 **"sprinkle semicolons"**: Sarah Boxer, *If Not Strong, At Least Tricky: The Middleweight of Punctuation Politics*, N.Y. Times (Mar. 6, 1999), https:// www.nytimes.com/1999/03/06/arts/think-tank-if-not-strong-at-least -tricky-the-middleweight-of-puctuation-politics.html.

## Chapter 11: Semicolons and Complex Lists

83 **"punctuate my joy"**: Buff Whitman-Bradley, *Semicolons of Anguish*, Atl. Rev. (Jan. 1, 2013).

84 **"Fred's favorite things"**: Patricia O'Conner, Woe Is I: The Grammarphobe's Guide to Better English in Plain English 194 (4th ed. 2019).

85 **"Thomas Jefferson"**: Jon Meacham, Thomas Jefferson: The Art of Power 437 (2012).

85 **"Winston Churchill"**: Winston Churchill, My Early Life: A Roving Commission 111 (1941).

85 **"Isaac Asimov":** Isaac Asimov, I, Asimov: A Memoir 117 (1979); *see also* Michael White, Isaac Asimov: A Life of the Grand Master of Science 84–85 (2005).

85 **"savage fierceness":** Edward Gibbon, The History of the Decline and Fall of the Roman Empire 4 (H. H. Milman ed., 1881).

86 **"The harm arose":** *State Farm Mut. Auto. Ins. Co. v. Campbell*, 538 U.S. 408, 426 (2003).

87 **"When items in series themselves contain commas":** Erika Suffern, *Serial Commas and Serial Semicolons*, MLA Style Center (June 15, 2017), https://style.mla.org/serial-commas-and-semicolons/.

87 **"bumped up":** *Semicolons, Colons, and Dashes*, Univ. of N.C. at Chapel Hill Writing Ctr., https://writingcenter.unc.edu/tips-and-tools/semi-colons-colons-and-dashes/ (last visited Apr. 26, 2021).

88 **"a matter of feeling":** Wayne C. Temple, Lincoln's Confidant: The Life of Noah Brooks 188 (Douglas L. Wilson & Rodney O. Davis eds., 2019).

90 **"Fred's favorite things":** Patricia O'Conner, Woe Is I: The Grammarphobe's Guide to Better English in Plain English 194 (4th ed. 2019).

## Chapter 12: Semicolon Deviation

91 **"half-assed semicolons":** Ursula K. Le Guin, The Wave in the Mind: Talks and Essays on the Writer, the Reader, and the Imagination 5 (2004).

92 **"Everyone on the mission had two specialties":** Andy Weir, The Martian 10 (Broadway Books 2014) (2011).

92 **"This man":** Frank O'Brien, *The Unknown Soldier*, N.Y. Herald (Nov. 11, 1921), at 8.

93 **"Punctuation rules aren't measures of our moral worth":** Dante Ramos, *The Period Is Dead—but So What?*, Bos. Globe (June 10, 2016, 3:34 P.M.), https://www.bostonglobe.com/opinion/2016/06/10/the-period-dead-but-what/igl5X3xVaa9d7gYAhY38HK/story.html.

93 **"millennials who omit periods":** *Id.*

94 **"wisely broken":** E. L. Thorndike, *The Psychology of Punctuation*, 61 Am. J. Psychol. 222 (1948).

94 **"promotion semicolon"**: Sarah Boxer, *If Not Strong, At Least Tricky: The Middleweight of Punctuation Politics*, N.Y. Times (Mar. 6, 1999), https://www.nytimes.com/1999/03/06/arts/think-tank-if-not-strong-at-least-tricky-the-middleweight-of-puctuation-politics.html.

94 **"a place where you can expect to sit for a moment, catching your breath"**: Lewis Thomas, The Medusa and the Snail: More Notes of a Biology Watcher 106 (1979).

95 **"Emma opposed this"**: Gustave Flaubert, Madame Bovary: Provincial Manners 70 (1856).

95 **"not here"**: Julian Barnes, Flaubert's Parrot 15 (1984).

95 **"a series of permissions"**: Susan Sontag, Where the Stress Falls 264 (2001).

95 **"leaving your family"**: Kiran Desai, The Inheritance of Loss 361 (2006).

## Chapter 13: Dependent Clauses

97 **"delight in dependent clauses"**: Leo Spitzer, *Zum Stil Marcel Proust's*, *in* Stilstudien 420 (1961).

98 **"mushrooms and semicolons"**: Richard Wydick, Plain English for Lawyers 90 (5th ed. 2005).

98 **"A clause is a grammatical unit"**: *Glossary of Grammatical Terms*, Oxford English Dictionary, https://public.oed.com/how-to-use-the-oed/glossary-grammatical-terms/#phrasal-verb (last visited Sept. 19, 2020).

99 **"Separate educational facilities are inherently unequal"**: *Brown v. Bd. of Educ.*, 347 U.S. 483, 495 (1954).

99 **"If it sounds like writing, I rewrite it"**: Elmore Leonard, *Easy on the Adverbs, Exclamation Points and Especially Hooptedoodle*, N.Y. Times (July 16, 2001), https://www.nytimes.com/2001/07/16/arts/writers-writing-easy-adverbs-exclamation-points-especially-hooptedoodle.html.

100 **"A dependent clause cannot stand on its own"**: Ila Tyagi, *Types of Clauses*, Yale Ctr. for Teaching & Learning, https://ctl.yale.edu/sites/default/files/files/Clauses_Updated_May_26_2015-1.pdf (last updated May 2015).

100    **"Some common dependent markers"**: *Identifying Independent and Dependent Clauses*, PURDUE ONLINE WRITING LAB, https://owl.purdue.edu/owl/general_writing/punctuation/independent_and_dependent_clauses/index.html (last visited Mar. 6, 2021).

100    **"The adverb clause"**: *Commas and Dependent Clauses*, UNIV. OF TEX. AT DALL. WRITING CTR., https://www.utdallas.edu/studentsuccess/files/Commas-and-Dependent-Clauses.pdf (last visited Mar. 6, 2021).

102    **"words are the surgeon's only tools"**: PAUL KALANITHI, WHEN BREATH BECOMES AIR 86–87 (Random House 2016).

102    **"A word after a word after a word"**: MARGARET ATWOOD: A WORD AFTER A WORD AFTER A WORD IS POWER (White Pine Pictures 2019).

102    **"I was going to have to write it"**: ANN PATCHETT, THE GETAWAY CAR: A PRACTICAL MEMOIR ABOUT WRITING AND LIFE 23 (Byliner Originals 2011).

102    **"create something that was not there"**: A LITANY FOR SURVIVAL: THE LIFE AND WORK OF AUDRE LORDE (Third World Newsreel 1995).

## Chapter 14: Isadora Duncan

105    **"methodical persistence"**: ELENA FERRANTE, THE STORY OF A NEW NAME 40 (2012).

106    **"I spent the morning taking out a comma, and the afternoon putting one back in"**: For a look into the origins of this phrase, see *I Spent All Morning Taking Out a Comma and All Afternoon Putting It Back*, QUOTE INVESTIGATOR (Oct. 25, 2015), https://quoteinvestigator.com/2015/10/25/comma.

107    **"prison of school"**: ISADORA DUNCAN, MY LIFE 2 (2013 Liveright) (1927).

109    **"Commas can help create the rhythm of a sentence"**: SOL STEIN, SOL STEIN'S REFERENCE BOOK FOR WRITERS 3 (2010).

109    **"Popping in a comma"**: Pico Iyer, *In Praise of the Humble Comma*, TIME (June 24, 2001), http://content.time.com/time/magazine/article/0,9171,149453,00.html.

109    **"Today, I learned, the comma"**: DANIEL KEYES, FLOWERS FOR ALGERNON 27 (Bantam ed. 1975) (1966).

110    **"disappears"**: SALMAN RUSHDIE, THE GROUND BENEATH HER FEET 519–20 (2001).

110   **"Leave a decent space of time"**: Zadie Smith, *Zadie Smith's Rules for Writers*, GUARDIAN (Feb. 22, 2010, 9:58 A.M.), theguardian.com/books/2010/feb/22/zadie-smith-rules-for-writers.

110   **"Omit needless words"**: WILLIAM STRUNK JR. & E. B. WHITE, THE ELEMENTS OF STYLE 32 (1959; 4th ed. 1999).

111   **"when people tell you something is wrong or it doesn't work for them"**: Neil Gaiman, *For All the People Who Ask Me for Writing Advice*, TUMBLR (May 7, 2012, 12:33 A.M.), https://neil-gaiman.tumblr.com/post/22573969110/for-all-the-people-who-ask-me-for-writing.

## Chapter 15: If-Then

113   **"There is truth and falsehood in the comma"**: TOM STOPPARD, THE INVENTION OF LOVE 37 (1997).

114   **"justice built into it"**: STEVEN STROGATZ, THE CALCULUS OF FRIENDSHIP: WHAT A TEACHER AND A STUDENT LEARNED ABOUT LIFE WHILE CORRESPONDING ABOUT MATH 6 (2009).

115   **"100 strands of spaghetti"**: *Id.* at 133.

115   **"Conditional clauses"**: *Conditionals*, CAMBRIDGE DICTIONARY, https://dictionary.cambridge.org/us/grammar/british-grammar/conditionals-and-wishes/conditionals (last visited Oct. 5, 2020).

116   **"When mathematicians and physicists are asked"**: STEVEN STROGATZ, THE JOY OF X: A GUIDED TOUR OF MATH, FROM ONE TO INFINITY 67 (2012).

117   **"Conditional sentences"**: *Zero Conditional*, BBC WORLD SERVICE GRAMMAR CHALLENGE, https://www.bbc.co.uk/worldservice/learningenglish/radio/specials/1636_gramchallenge22/ (last visited Apr. 19, 2021).

117   **"require commas to separate"**: *If, Then Statements Require Commas*, CONSTANT CONTENT (Dec. 12, 2007), https://www.constant-content.com/content-writing-service/2007/12/if-then-statements-require-commas/.

117   **"When readability"**: Douglas B. West, *The Grammar according to West*, UNIV. OF ILL. AT URBANA-CHAMPAIGN, https://faculty.math.illinois.edu/~west/gramwest.pdf (last visited Apr. 19, 2021).

118   **"real world as a theorem"**: DOUGLAS HOFSTADTER, GÖDEL, ESCHER, BACH: AN ETERNAL GOLDEN BRAID 254 (1979).

118 **"My investigation"**: Margot Lee Shetterly, Hidden Figures: The American Dream and the Untold Story of the Black Women Mathematicians Who Helped Win the Space Race xvii (2016).

## Epilogue

121 **"with punctuation in the right places"**: Raymond Carver, *A Storyteller's Shoptalk*, N.Y. Times (Feb. 15, 1981), https://archive.nytimes.com/www .nytimes.com/books/01/01/21/specials/carver-shoptalk.html.

# PHOTO CREDITS

### Chapter 1

Dbenbenn. "Stop Sign." Available in the public domain. https:// commons.wikimedia.org/wiki/File:Stop_sign.png.

Fry1989. "United States Sign—Yield." Available in the public domain. https://commons.wikimedia.org/wiki/File:United_States_sign_ -_Yield_(v3).svg.

### Chapter 3

Gardner, Alexander. "Abraham Lincoln Head on Shoulders Photo Portrait." Available in the public domain. https://commons .wikimedia.org/wiki/File:Abraham_Lincoln_head_on_shoulders _photo_portrait.jpg.

"Angelou at Clinton Inauguration." William J. Clinton Presidential Library. Available in the public domain. https://commons .wikimedia.org/wiki/File:Angelou_at_Clinton_inauguration.jpg.

### Chapter 4

Popova, Maria. "Oliver Sacks." Licensed under CC BY-SA 3.0. https://commons.wikimedia.org/wiki/File:Oliversacks.jpg.

Lara, Jose. "Gabriel Garcia Marquez." Licensed under CC BY-SA 2.0. https://commons.wikimedia.org/wiki/File:Gabriel_Garcia _Marquez.jpg.

## Chapter 5

"John Updike with Bushes New." George Bush Presidential Library. Available in the public domain. https://commons.wikimedia.org/ wiki/File:John_Updike_with_Bushes_new.jpg.

## Chapter 6

"Jhumpa Lahiri." Librairie Mollat. Licensed under CC BY 3.0. https:// commons.wikimedia.org/wiki/File:Jhumpa_Lahiri_(2015).png.

Albertin, Walter. "E. E. Cummings." Available in the public domain. https://commons.wikimedia.org/wiki/File:E._E._Cummings _NYWTS.jpg.

## Chapter 7

Petteway, Steve. "Official Roberts CJ." Available in the public domain. https://commons.wikimedia.org/wiki/File:Official_roberts_CJ .jpg.

## Chapter 9

D'Albert Durade, François. "George Elliot." National Portrait Gallery. Available in the public domain. https://commons.wikimedia.org/ wiki/File:George_Eliot,_por_Fran%C3%A7ois_D%27Albert _Durade.jpg.

William Blackwood & Sons. "Middlemarch 1." Available in the public domain. https://commons.wikimedia.org/wiki/File:Middlemarch _1.jpg.

PBS. "Kurt Vonnegut 1972." Available in the public domain. https:// en.wikipedia.org/wiki/File:Kurt_Vonnegut_1972.jpg.

## Chapter 11

Reynolds, Joshua. "Edward Emily Gibbon." Available in the public domain. https://commons.wikimedia.org/wiki/File:Edward_Emily_Gibbon.jpg.

Oyez Project. "Anthony Kennedy, Official SCOTUS Portrait." Available in the public domain. https://commons.wikimedia.org/wiki/File:Anthony_Kennedy_official_SCOTUS_portrait.jpg.

## Chapter 14

Nadar. "Gustave Flaubert." Available in the public domain. https://commons.wikimedia.org/wiki/File:Gustave_Flaubert.jpg.

W. & D. Downey. "Oscar Wilde." Available in the public domain. https://commons.wikimedia.org/wiki/File:Oscar_Wilde_(1854-1900)_1889,_May_23._Picture_by_W._and_D._Downey.jpg.

Baker Art Gallery. "Isadora Duncan." Available in the public domain. https://commons.wikimedia.org/wiki/File:Isadora_Duncan_-_first_fairy.jpg.

CPSIA information can be obtained
at www.ICGtesting.com
Printed in the USA
JSHW012131280423
41038JS00007B/80